JOSHUA CUNNINGHAM

ADVENTURE CYCLING, BIKEPACKING
AND TOURING OFF-ROAD

WITH OVER 200 ILLUSTRATIONS

ESCAPE

BY

BIKE

 Thames & Hudson

CONTENTS

OVERLAND

BY

BIKE

'Adventure cycling', 'cycle touring', 'bikepacking', 'bike travel', 'bike tripping', 'bike bivvying': there's an ever-increasing list of sub-genres that people like to use when talking about travelling by bike, and the nuances differentiating a touring cyclist from a cycle tourist are very much real, but we are all essentially people on bikes, with bags attached, pedalling from one point to another, and that's what matters.

Whether a multi-year, circumnavigational epic, a summertime jaunt spread across a couple of weeks or months, or a one-night wander spent enjoying the local roads or trails, ultimately, it's all the same. It's about evoking a sense of freedom, experiencing a rawness of life, meeting new people, exploring places you otherwise wouldn't, and getting to know them in a way that most travellers only dream of.

As a teenager I spent consecutive summers doing just that, initiating myself into the world of cycle touring by exploring portions of Europe with friends – mostly Pete and Rob, who joined me for much of the year-long journey from Dumfries to Hong Kong that this book follows. As a trio or part of larger groups, we cycled to Italy, then to Amsterdam, and crammed in shorter excursions around the UK as and when we could: a motley crew of spotty pipsqueaks, riding decrepit mountain bikes and wearing gargantuan hiking rucksacks, crammed with any camping equipment we could get our hands on, experiencing whatever places and people came our way from one day to the next. These experiences would form the basis for a near-unquenchable thirst for cycling adventure, and I was completely unaware of it at the time. The cycle-touring seed had been planted.

It wouldn't be until a number of years had passed that we again found ourselves in the midst of another cycling adventure – except this time our rendezvous point would be in Dushanbe, the capital of Tajikistan. It was June 2015, a year that I spent cycling from the UK to Hong Kong, on a journey that would take me through 26 countries and across 21,000 km (over 13,000 miles of

ON P. 2 Heading into the foothills of the Himalayas from the hot flatlands of the Punjab, India.
ON P. 4 Morning light in the Agordino valley, Italian Dolomites.
PREVIOUS PAGES Dusk in the Tien Shan mountains, Kyrgyzstan.

the Eurasian landmass in an almost unbroken trail of pedalling. In a romantic testament to our early years of haphazardly navigating the cycle-touring landscape, Pete and Rob joined me for much of the way.

The culture

Bike touring began in its earliest form during the second half of the 19th century, not long after the velocipede, as it was known, had been invented. Members of newly fashionable bicycle clubs began venturing out on multi-day excursions, between cities and into the countryside, on their rickety, uncomfortable contraptions. These pioneers of adventure cycling carried a few essentials in rolled-up packs attached to their handlebars, or in suitcases strapped on top of a primitive rack.

Before long the velocipedes evolved into penny-farthings, whose oversized front wheels afforded a far greater travelling speed, and the gentle excursions developed into intercontinental forays as cyclists began to explore Europe and America by bike.

It was inevitable that an around-the-world journey would be next, and it was a Brit, Thomas Stevens, who was the first to accomplish it after setting out across the USA in 1884. Initially planning just a cross-country stint from San Francisco to Boston, Stevens struck up a sponsorship deal upon finishing his 100-day adventure and set about planning its continuation. Two years later, he ended his journey in Japan, having cycled over 20,000 km (12,400 miles) across Europe, the Middle East, India and the Far East aboard a penny-farthing to get there.

Today bicycle touring, from transcontinental hauls to brief bikepacking blitzes, is enjoying a popularity far at odds with even just a few years ago, let alone the time of trailblazers like Thomas Stevens. We live in an age when advances in technology and ease of international travel are making the world an ever-smaller place and, as a result, more and more people are taking to their bikes to see it for themselves. These modern adventurers come from road-cycling or mountain-biking backgrounds, or backgrounds that involve no cycling whatsoever, but all are unified by the prospect of combining cycling and travel. They want to recapture the mystique of our planet, attempt to fill in the gaps that escape the automated transport experience and discover the secrets that bicycle travel unlocks.

'It is by riding a bicycle that you learn the contours of a country best, since you have to sweat up the hills and coast down them,' wrote Ernest Hemingway, himself a keen cyclist. 'Thus you remember them as they actually are, while in a motor car only a high hill impresses you, and you have no such accurate remembrance of the country you have driven through as you gain by riding a bicycle.'

This level of understanding doesn't strictly relate to topography either. Sure, the impression that Hemingway gives is of a physical incline in the road underneath him, but a country's contours are myriad. Two wheels will indeed grant you a self-earned passage through some of the most spectacular landscapes the world has to offer, but they also provide a portal into the varied experience of life on earth. In realizing that, the nuances between a cyclist on a tour and a tourist on a cycle become clear, and the multifaceted nature of an adventure cycling journey can be enjoyed to its full.

Assuming that, having got this far, you are one of these adventurers, you will find plenty of practical advice peppered throughout this book, providing insight into all aspects of adventure cycling and making getting out there yourself as irresistible as possible.

What's to come

Each of the five chapters that follows focuses on a different environment (forests, mountains, deserts, tropics and cities), defined by the varying climates and related experiences those embarking on an adventure-cycling tour will be most likely to encounter. My own crossing of Eurasia took in each of them, and the chapters proceed chronologically across their elemental boundaries.

From my experiences I've extrapolated what I found defined in each of these climates, and what would be translatable to other, similar environments around the world, from both a cyclist's and a traveller's perspective. In this respect, I hope that the book allows for a certain amount of vicarious experience, enabling you to apply it to your own cycling adventure. It also offers tips on things like bike and equipment choices, wild camping and navigating the red tape that comes with long-distance overland travel.

Starting in the forests of Europe – paying special attention to cold-weather touring owing to my own winter departure (but also reflecting on the climatic variation of the temperate zone, and its suitability for beginners) – the journey gradually thaws as it makes its way east. The deserts and heat of Kazakhstan and Uzbekistan form the basis of chapter two, before the appearance of the Himalayas provide an excuse to explore the mountains in chapter three. As the journey progresses through the Indian Subcontinent and South East Asia, you'll be well and truly immersed in the tropical heat of chapter four, before the melting pot that is Hong Kong provides a fitting end to the journey.

As it navigates through the chapters, the book explores the differences in climate, remoteness, altitude, population density and road surface between the regions, and what effect they have on the cycling experience. You'll discover the different kinds of cycle touring and adventure cycling and the bikes and setups associated with each, and realize that none of these are set in stone. If you want to drag a 50 kg (110 lbs) bike with 32 mm (1¼ in.) slick tyres up a 4,000 m (13,120 ft) pass on a rocky, unmade track, you certainly can (chapter three has plenty of examples). But you'll also learn that with appropriately tailored bikes and gear, struggles are minimized and enjoyment heightened to the full.

You'll discover what you need to take with you, what you need to be able to ride, sleep and cook in relative comfort, how to navigate, stay healthy and transport and

OVERLEAF Spiti valley, Himachal Pradesh, India. **ON P. 16** Evening climb on the Rohtang Pass.

look after your bike. Along with the physical differences in environment that cycle touring will expose you to, you'll also get a feel for the scope of introspective experiences it offers: the differences between shorter and longer journeys and between having a partner and riding solo, or the figurative mountains it will enable you to conquer.

Of course, all of this will become clearer once you've departed on your cycling adventure and found out for yourself – once you've felt your stomach churn over with every emotion you've ever known, slept in a roadside ditch and woke up thinking nothing of it, experienced the innate kindness of people around the world, dragged your bike to the top of an unpaved mountain pass or thought for the tenth time that day: 'That's the best view I've ever seen in my life.'

What follows is a journal of my experiences, as well as a representation of the slice of Planet Earth that I discovered on my cycling adventure. Hopefully, it will play a part in helping you to discover yours.

1

FORESTS

DUMFRIES, UK – BAKU, AZERBAIJAN

- CHOOSING THE RIGHT BIKE: TRADITIONAL
- PREPARATION AND PAPERWORK
- CYCLING IN COLD WEATHER
- ALONE OR WITH A COMPANION?
- SLEEPING AND SHELTER
- TRAINING

DUMFRIES, UK – BAKU, AZERBAIJAN

7,000 KM (4,350 MILES), JANUARY–APRIL

UK, FRANCE, BELGIUM, LUXEMBOURG, GERMANY,
AUSTRIA, ITALY, SLOVENIA, CROATIA, BOSNIA &
HERZEGOVINA, MONTENEGRO, ALBANIA, MACEDONIA,
GREECE, TURKEY, GEORGIA, AZERBAIJAN

TERRAIN: **TARMAC, GRAVEL**

FEATURED BIKE: **TRADITIONAL TOURER**

MOST VALUED ITEM OF KIT: **DOWN JACKET**

AFTER TWO DAYS OF CLIMBING,

we eventually arrive at the summit of the Goderdzi Pass
in southern Georgia, in the falling snow and failing light
of early evening. The road we have been following has
been dug out between two walls of snow, visibility is
reduced to 6 or 9 m (20 or 30 ft), a rusty Soviet obelisk
looms through the mist, and the obligatory wild dog limps
around between our wheels. Out of the gloom a group of
men appears, one armed with a shotgun, who demand
first some photos and then that we join them for some
vodka. We decline the vodka, but pose reluctantly with a
bird of prey that has presumably just been killed.

The descent, once we begin it, proves to be far worse
than the climb. The road remains an unsealed mixture
of rock and sand, and the snow grows steadily heavier.
Having forgotten the cold on the ascent, its bite is now

intolerable as we sit motionless on our saddles, feeling our hands stiffen into claws around the brake levers. After two stops to adjust them, my brake pads eventually wear out completely, and I am left dragging my foot along the ground in a vain effort to reduce speed. Clacking over the rocky ground, with a full tug on the brakes reducing speed by approximately 0 kmh, and the snow blinding us as we navigate our way slowly down, it feels as though refuge – in whatever form – will never materialize.

After 45 km (28 miles) the tarmac eventually begins again, just before the town of Adigeni, and we roll into it at 8pm, in darkness. With the snow unrelenting, we make for the first abandoned building we see and immediately change out of our riding gear into down jackets and fleeces. We put up the tent in the basement, but on closer inspection discover that the floor is made of congealed cow shit. In the corner are the unmistakable signs that it had been used by humans for a similar purpose. A bat appears from the rafters and begins to flap all over the place, while the silhouette of a stray dog scuttles past the entrance of our home for the night.

Despite this unpromising beginning, it takes all of five seconds to decide to stay: there's too much snow, and we're too cold, hungry and tired to move on. Our impromptu refuge, mysteriously absent from the Lonely Planet guide, will have to do for the night.

• • •

Temperate zones form a broad, loosely defined segment of the planet stretching roughly between the latitudes that separate the tropics from the poles. They can, despite the name, provide highly changeable environments for bike touring, from harsh winters to hot summers. As much of Europe and parts of the US, the Far East and the Southern Hemisphere fall under this umbrella, this is where many cyclists are introduced to bike touring. With the varied experiences the temperate zones offer, there are few better places for it.

CHOOSING THE RIGHT BIKE:

On a cycle tour, especially self-supported ones, your bike effectively becomes your home. If you're not riding it, then you're sleeping next to it, talking about it, rummaging through bags attached to it or looking at it propped up against a tree while you eat something that until that point was being transported by it. The bike is you, and you are the bike. This symbiotic relationship must be respected, and that means choosing a bike that will help keep both sides of the relationship happy.

There is no definitive way of categorizing bike-touring setups, and personalizing your bike is to be encouraged. The lines of tradition are continually being blurred as cyclists experiment with new combinations of bike, luggage and equipment. Essentially, however, there are five setup categories: traditional, expedition, mountain, extreme and ultralight. Depending on your tour's duration and location, the basic principles of each – or a combination of them – can be used as a starting point from which to build your bike.

TRADITIONAL

Most people get into cycle touring via the 'traditional' cycle-touring setup, ideal for shorter tours in a stable climate. The basic requirement is that you have a bit of extra space to carry some essentials on a multi-day excursion – spare clothes, perhaps, and some sort of sleeping arrangement – and a comfortable road bike on which to roll.

For a breakdown of kit lists for a range of tours, see pp. 260–1.

1. STEEL FRAME

Extremely hardwearing, with the perfect balance of comfort and efficiency. Handbuilt custom frames are an option for those with deep pockets and who are after an extra-special bond with their bike. Just make sure there are eyelets for mounting racks, and mudguards.

2. COMFORTABLE GEOMETRY

The long wheelbase provides stability and helps to absorb bumps when your bike is loaded up with panniers. A taller head tube offers more height at the front end, reducing stress on the back during long hours in the saddle.

3. DROP HANDLEBARS

These provide a range of hand positions for optimal comfort and stability when climbing, descending or breezing along. Consider fitting an extra pair of brake levers on top for added control.

4. SINGLE-PANNIER LUGGAGE SYSTEM

For shorter tours, one set of flap-top or roll-top panniers is fine. These are usually fitted at the rear, but fitting them at the front, too, can increase stability. A small front rack or handlebar bag is al so useful for valuables.

5. CANTILEVER BRAKES

Providing a strong and effective rim-brake system, 'canties' are easy to maintain and have readily sourceable components.

6. 700C WHEELS

For light touring on mostly tarmac roads, 25–35 mm (1–1¼ in.) 700c tyres will provide the perfect combination of speed and comfort.

7. GOOD GEAR RANGE

A triple or compact double chainset at the front, coupled with a regular 12–28, 9 or 10-speed cassette at the rear, will give you every gear ratio you'll need.

8. STI SHIFTERS

STI shifters, where the brakes and gears are housed in the same unit, are ergonomic and a ubiquitous feature of the modern tour-orientated road bike.

PREPARATION
AND
PAPERWORK

In the months prior to your departure, the less glamorous administrative side of the journey will need to be addressed. Once you're out exploring the world, the only thing you're going to want to think about is the riding, so it's best to take care of as much of the boring stuff as possible before you leave. Visas and travel permits are the biggest barrier to unbroken overland travel and the hoops required for successful applications change constantly, but here are some points to consider:

Do you need to apply for anything at embassies before leaving?
Are there more than six months remaining on your passport?
Will you need letters from employers or proof of address?
Will the presence of other visas in your passport delay approval of your application and/or affect the order in which you apply for visas?
How many passport photos will you need?
How long does the application procedure take, and when do you need to begin it?

Are you obliged to arrive on the date you stated in your application?
Does the country you plan to visit have embassies where you can make your application on the road, and do the requirements change between them?
What currencies can you pay fees in?
Do the start and end dates of each visa overlap, and do they allow enough time to travel across the whole country?
Is there a registration procedure for the country you want to visit? What are the consequences if you fail to follow it?
Will you need to employ the services of a visa agent?
What happens if your planned route closes because of bureaucracy?
Do you have a Plan B?
And most importantly: is your information current?

As far as **insurance** goes, keep in mind that while cycle touring isn't quite in the realms of mountaineering or arctic exploration, as far as an insurer is concerned, it might as well be. Policies are riddled with clauses that play with the definition of cycle touring, and what is or isn't covered. There are differences in potential risk between an overnighter to Liverpool and a week in the Levant, and your insurance could be void if you travel to places discouraged by your country's foreign office. The best advice would be to accept that you're not going to cover everything. If you do choose to be adventurous, your wellbeing, your stuff and your bank balance could pay the price.

Depending on the location and time of year, you are as likely to find yourself riding through snowstorms in sub-zero temperatures as cruising beneath a glowing sun, with a warm breeze in the air and the spine-tingling anticipation of a night under the stars. Having left the UK during a snowy January, and then ridden through the Mediterranean and across Turkey and the Caucasus when spring was just beginning to emerge, I had experienced the full spectrum of conditions.

Barely a week into my year-long trip, cycling through Belgium in the snow and plummeting overnight temperatures of a European winter, I had sought out a barn as a potential refuge in the darkness.

'Bonjour, madame, c'est possible...,' I began hesitantly, staging a pantomime of sleeping and pointing, as the elderly owner stood silently in the doorway of the adjoining house, with the warm glow of a farmhouse kitchen radiating behind her.

'Oui,' she said eventually, looking me up and down, evidently bemused by my snow-blasted, bedraggled appearance. Her assent was typical of the unconditional kindness I would often be the grateful recipient of throughout my journey.

After unzipping the tent the following morning, I discovered to my dismay that beyond the gloom of the barn, which had obviously long ceased functioning as a farm building, it was still snowing. A good few inches had fallen overnight, making me even more grateful for the roof above my tent. Although the prospect of pulling on my clothes, frozen stiff after being left hanging outside the tent overnight, was unappealing, the winter wonderland outside was enough to whet my appetite for the day ahead. I had been away for less than a week, but already the adventure felt as though it engulfed me.

Before I had set off on my journey, it was these experiences that I craved, but that had sometimes, while I was saving up and seeing out prior commitments, seemed as though they would forever belong to other people. I had spent years reading the blogs of other cycle tourists as

CYCLING IN
COLD WEATHER

Double gloves (a glove liner, with a roomy winter glove like a skiing mitt over the top) are often the best way of insulating your hands.

Pogies (large mittens that attach permanently to your handlebars) are worth looking at if the weather is very extreme.

Good socks: Sealskinz offer a sock with a plastic membrane in it, which acts as a waterproof and insulative layer, but a basic woollen sock (or layered socks) is a tried and tested alternative.

Inflatable mattresses offer much more insulation than foam versions. Your body loses most of its heat into the ground, rather than into the surrounding air.

Keep sweat to a minimum as much as possible, as getting clothes completely dry is difficult and the damp will feel colder once your body cools down.

Try to camp on a bed of snow, rather than on frozen ground, to make the best use of the insulation it provides.

Keep your clothes dry and bring any that get damp, such as socks or base layers, into your sleeping bag at night to prevent them from freezing stiff.

Store bottles in your panniers during the day, as they will freeze solid if kept in bottle cages.

Spiked tyres: if roads are icy, consider fitting spiked tyres, such as Schwalbe's Ice Spiker range.

Think about toilet arrangements: during the night, find a system (such as an empty bottle) that means you don't have to re-emerge at any point to pee.

Use a petrol stove, as gas can be unreliable in cold temperatures.

Eat, eat, eat: your body will be burning thousands of calories each day just to function and keep warm. Add a day of cycling to that, and you're left with a big calorie deficit that needs to be replenished.

Be prepared for breakages: cold weather makes some materials brittle and fragile, and the grime your bike picks up from melted slush and grit can wreak havoc on its moving parts.

they embarked on adventures around the world, eagerly waiting for updates and reading their stories from far-flung places. Knowing that these experiences were out there, waiting to be discovered, but feeling intimidated by the prospect of making the leap in search of them, is normal. Leaving on an adventure – especially a big one – is always the most difficult part. Once you have set off, however, there is very little difference between an overnight tour and a transcontinental one. Each passing day becomes merely an extension of a sequence of experiences that quickly erode previous worries. Will I be safe? Will I be fit enough? What if my campsite is discovered? Will I be able to find food and water when I need it?

As time begins to pass in a whirlwind of new sensations and scenarios, there is little time to dwell on anything. Each new addition to the experience bank builds on the foundations of those before it, and makes the next a little less alien. Like everyone else, leaving was a big one for me, and that barn in Belgium became a key part of those foundations – its dilapidated, neglected shell redefined as an integral part of my adventure-cycling apprenticeship.

Cold weather has an impact in any circumstances, but when spending extended periods outside on your bike, it completely governs them. Your sense of practicality and survival instinct are attuned to the extreme, and every decision revolves around the question: 'What effect will this action have on my body temperature?'

It becomes quickly apparent, especially while camping, that there are usually only two scenarios in which achieving some sort of thermal comfort is possible: when pedalling, or when in your sleeping bag and unconscious. Activities like eating, taking photos or covering the short distance between your bike and the warmth of a shop become missions of absolute efficiency to prevent the cold from seeping in. It's relentless and draining, and becomes more difficult the more time is spent without a building to sleep in (these usually came every few nights in the shape of a Warm Showers host; p. 258). But while challenging, travelling self-supported through the cold is also invigorating, providing a rare opportunity to reacquaint your 21st-century self with the primal instincts that get forgotten about in the monotony of daily life – even if they are only fully enjoyed in retrospect.

After three weeks of enduring the cold, I reached the Mediterranean. While cycling through Italy, Slovenia, Croatia, Macedonia and Greece, I began to enjoy a pleasant coastal microclimate, despite it still being winter. The day-to-day comfort it permitted, from being warm and dry to the reduced stress on bike and gear, was echoed in the sprightliness of the silhouette projected back at me from the tarmac. The winter sun, despite being unable to hoist itself much higher than the surrounding cliffs, felt warm on my back, and I chased the shadow it cast in front of me for as long as I could each day, enjoying this perfect introduction to cycle touring.

Temperate forest regions are often densely populated and seasonally touristy, and Europe was no exception. While this has its benefits, including ample supplies and never being too far from a bike shop or hospital, it has its detractions, too. I found that I had to plan my wild camps around towns along the road, and more often than not would pitch up in disused industrial estates, behind petrol stations, in drainage culverts or some similarly unattractive locale, rather than more picturesque locations, where discovery would be much more likely.

At dusk I would quickly nip into a shop and pick up supplies, before heading out the other side of the town and finding a spot to camp. If I couldn't get in and out of town before dark, I'd make do with the supplies I kept on me (which in expensive Europe meant bread, cheese and ketchup – the 'hobo pizza') and content myself with the knowledge that breakfast would only be a short ride away in the morning. It was a far cry from the remote expanses of the desert, mountains and jungle I would experience later on, where wild camping was as easy as rolling my bike off the road and pitching up at whatever point I decided I'd had enough for the day.

ALONE OR WITH A COMPANION?

The experience of six weeks alone on a bike opened my eyes to the benefits of solo bike travel.

Our basic need for human contact means that you, as a solo traveller, are much more likely to introduce yourself to people and enter into conversation, and that you become more approachable to others. **In periods spent on my own in Europe, and later in Uzbekistan, India and the** Far East, I found myself spending much more time with locals, usually after having been invited to join a group having lunch, or into someone's home.

In any group, big or small, you immediately become less approachable, and you will have lost some of the vulnerability that might have drawn people towards you. Having said that, there are few occasions where safety in numbers doesn't count for something.

You are more fast-moving on your own, without having to worry about the needs of someone else. But a second opinion can be invaluable on the road, from route-planning to deciding whether or not to beat a hasty retreat from a situation.

The mental comfort given by the presence of another person is priceless, whether for sharing moments of joy or suffering, or reminiscing together at a later date.

SLEEPING AND SHELTER

Like your bike, your shelter can be optimized for the type of tour you want to embark on, depending on length or climate, or how self-supported it will be. In general, there are three options:

1. TENT

For longer tours through multiple climates, or at a time of year when the weather is unpredictable, a tent is probably the best option. Features to look out for include the dimensions and weight of the packed tent, which will give you an idea of how easy it will be to transport and what sort of luggage you'll need to carry it. Consider, also, the colour: will it blend into your surroundings and minimize your chances of being disturbed? Porches are useful for storing luggage and smelly shoes outside of the inner fly, and a geodesic or semi-geodesic design (where the tent is able to support itself) is a big advantage when camping in places where tent pegs can't be driven into the ground. A supported inner fly is useful when the weather is hot, giving you a cool space to sleep in and protection from wildlife. And lastly, if you're bringing a tent, you're clearly not too bothered about weight and speed, so do yourself a favour and get a tent with some room: 1-person tour = 2-person tent; 2-person tour = 3-person tent, and so on.

2. TARP

Tarp-camping is divisive among cycle tourists. Some people swear by it, others can't bear the faff involved in erecting one. Once mastered, however, a tarp is a lightweight and practical way of providing shelter. It will keep you dry in all but the harshest conditions, and condense down into a neat little package. It is often used in conjunction with a hammock, which usually requires the same kind of sturdy fixed point to attach it to, and is a good halfway house between the confines of a closed tent and the exposure of a bivvy bag.

3. BIVVY BAG

Sleeping in a bivvy bag is perhaps the purest way of sleeping in the great outdoors. Modern bivvy bags are incredibly light and portable, and, when combined with an appropriate sleeping bag, provide ample protection against the cold and wet. If the weather turns, you might have an uncomfortable night, but if it remains clear and bright, you will, quite literally, be sleeping under the stars. When it comes to your sleeping bag, the most important thing to consider is the temperature range it was designed for. Winter tours in sub-zero temperatures will require a four- or five-season bag for comfort, but the same bag will be too much in the heat of the tropics or the desert. If your tour encompasses both of these climates, then opt for comfort in the cold, as you can always ditch the sleeping bag if it gets too hot. Silk or cotton liners are a good idea, as they will save you having to wash the entire sleeping bag. The most important item of all – your camping mattress – comes in two forms: inflatable and non-inflatable. Inflatable mattresses offer extra padding and insulation, which can make all the difference on a cold night. The drawback is that they are prone to splits and punctures, leading some long-distance tourers to revert back to non-inflatable foam roll-ups.

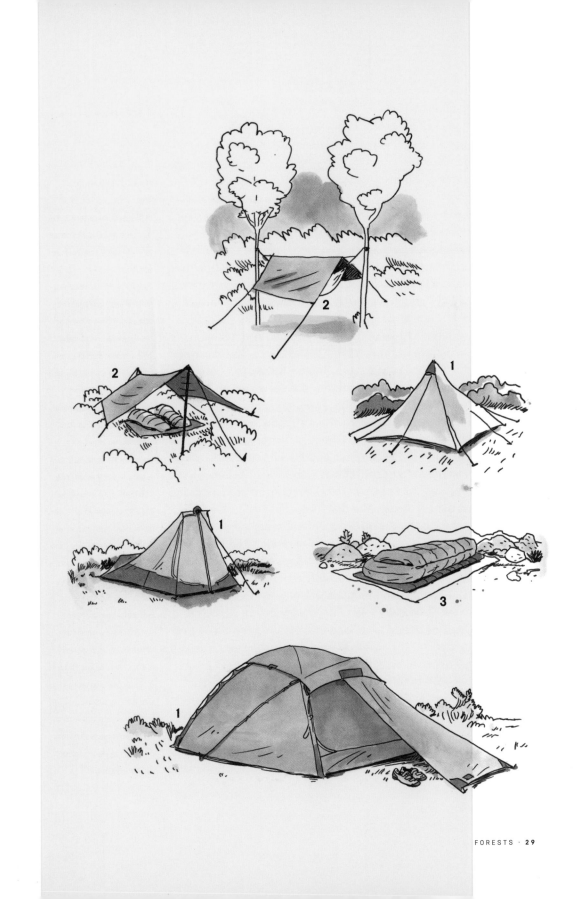

My route took me into Bosnia and Herzegovina, through Sarajevo, where the evidence of war was still very visible, and south towards the Montenegrin border. The abandoned, bullet-ridden buildings, the cold and the loneliness of travelling solo for the last month made the UK feel very far away, and the rawness of this new environment had begun to cause a stirring of trepidation. Because of the rumours of thousands of unexploded landmines in Bosnia, I decided to ask some locals if I could camp on their property. Such exchanges, although brief and without fuss, could rectify even the most sullen of moods simply through a smile and the mental break from having to find somewhere safe to sleep.

Once in Turkey, I met up with Rob. Having begun our respective journeys in the UK and Sweden, we were now due to head east as one, across Turkey, the Caucasus and Central Asia, giving me both a travelling partner for the next few months, and somebody to tackle the run-in to Istanbul with. The struggles required to haul ourselves through the European winter had taken their toll, but the brief communications we had shared ('I'm in a McDonald's near Bratislava, don't want to leave, can't feel toes') had been morale-boosting, somehow making us a team despite the distance.

After an hour or so of excitable conversation, we hauled ourselves back into our saddles and poked our noses into the wind towards Istanbul. Six weeks of exposure to the elements had left me with permanently numb toes, blistered lips and an insistent grumbling cough, and I needed the comforts I imagined Istanbul would bring. Once we crossed the Bosphorus, leaving the cosmopolitan ancient city and its historical ties with Europe behind us, we were ready to experience the Asiatic unknown.

Minarets calling the faithful to prayer and remnants of the personality cult surrounding Mustafa Kemal Atatürk, the first president of Turkey, were signs that our journey had moved into unfamiliar territory. Great swathes of emptiness stretched out on either side of the road, halfway between steppe and rolling pasture; snow-capped hills

TRAINING

Many people assume they could never go on an adventure bike tour, citing a lack of physical fitness or the necessary mental aptitude. But there is an easy way of overcoming this: if you can cycle to the end of the street, you could cycle to the next town. If you can continue to the next town, you could probably keep going a bit further, before doing the same the next day. If you keep doing that, over multiple days, you'll have covered hundreds of kilometres and gone on a bike tour. Even if you can only manage 20 km (12 miles) on the first day, your body will soon adapt. Your mental attitude requires merely that you welcome the graft and remain open-minded. What is most important is that you're comfortable on the bike, so make sure you get experience riding it beforehand to uncover any problems with your position or the mechanics of the bike itself.

and distant mosques peppered the horizon and flocks of sheep or goats, tended by a solitary figure leaning on a staff, intermittently populated the middle distance. Everything had grown in size and receded in proximity since leaving Europe, and we began to feel increasingly insignificant in the open, featureless landscape. It would be a taste of things to come.

It was still March, and the high plateau of inland Turkey, followed by the mountain passes of southern Georgia, were still in winter's thrall, their relatively lofty heights having not yet been painted with the same springtime brush the Mediterranean had been. Having tasted the ease and comfort of riding in those warmer southern climes, I had become weary of the cold. After being buffeted between climatic extremes of the temperate forest for the last three months, the Goderdzi Pass thankfully proved a final flirtation with winter for a while. As we continued east into the lowlands of the Caucasus, the sun's presence began, at long last, to be felt.

As in Greece, Macedonia and Croatia, camping in these temperate regions, with their ample water supplies and moderate temperatures, meant that being outside became a genuine pleasure again. The warm hues and long shadows that filtered through the tent in the mornings signalled the start of a day to be enjoyed, rather than endured, and we took our time brewing coffee and eating breakfast in whatever patch of countryside had taken our fancy the previous evening.

The kilometres breezed by during the day, and the late-afternoon sun, which faded so subtly into dusk that we were often left scrambling for a campsite before the light disappeared, was accompanied by the sights and sounds of people enjoying the first days of spring: sat out in front of their houses, socializing with their neighbours, collecting water, tending crops and telling their children to stop pestering the foreigners who had suddenly appeared. As the trip went on, riding at dusk would be eternally associated with these few days in the Caucasus.

'Azerbaijan border – Good luck!' read the sign above the road, as we approached the country's northern border with Georgia, nestled at the foot of the Caucasus mountains. The capital, Baku, has visa-issuing embassies for both Uzbekistan and Tajikistan, as well as a port from which a voyage across the Caspian Sea to Kazakhstan could – after some stressful negotiating of logistics – be made. In short, Azerbaijan held the key to unlocking our onward route, clearing it of bureaucracy until China. So while noting the sign with a smile, we nonetheless felt that some luck was needed.

At some point between the border and Baku, the green pastures of the Georgian spring gave way to parched scrublands. The yellow soil was held together with meagre scraps of vegetation, and the sun shone with an intensity we had not yet encountered. Thermal outer layers were replaced with sweat and sun cream, while the eternal hunger that went along with keeping warm was replaced with the eternal thirst that went with keeping cool. The deserts lying just on the other side of the Caspian Sea felt perceptibly close, and it seemed, having experienced both its wintry extreme and easygoing, cycle-friendly warmth, that we were leaving the temperate forest region behind us for good.

Now it was up to the deserts, mountains and tropics to take us deeper into the extremes.

ABOVE On tour, packing and unpacking your kit every day becomes second nature. **LEFT** Climbing through the mist near the town of Siran on the Turkish plateau. **RIGHT** The final few switchbacks of the Zigana Pass in the Pontic Alps, Turkey. **ON P. 33** Riding into the first days of spring in Azerbaijan.

Making slow progress on the Goderdzi Pass in southern Georgia,
which links Khulo with Adigeni in the Lesser Caucasus mountain range.

ABOVE Aboard the ferry across the Bosphorus and poring over maps, accompanied by a glass of Turkish *çay* (tea).
RIGHT Asking a baffled young Azerbaijani boy for directions.
LEFT On the Croatian coast, enjoying the winter sun.
OVERLEAF The other-worldly rock formations of Cappadocia, Turkey.

Making use of an abandoned
building for extra shelter on a
particularly windy night along
the Croatian coast. In spite
of the wind, eating dinner
underneath the stars offers a
moment of peace and a chance
to take stock of the day.

ABOVE Mudguards and roads formed of sticky clay proved to be a bad mix.
RIGHT A hot drink to ward off the crisp morning chill.
OVERLEAF Dawn breaks on another day on the road, just outside of Tbilisi, in Georgia. Spring is just beginning to make an appearance.

ABOVE Finding somewhere to camp is a skill honed over time. Once mastered, it can result in some unique and wonderful 'bedrooms'.
LEFT One-pot wonders are a staple of camp life.
RIGHT Rob's hands show the effects of spending all day outside and the general wear and tear of life on the road.
OVERLEAF Emerging through the mist in Germany, these trees seem to capture the cold and loneliness of riding through a European winter.

ABOVE Descending from the Lesser Caucasus into Gori, Georgia, birthplace of Joseph Stalin.
LEFT Much of Turkey's high-altitude interior is littered with long, gradual mountain passes.
RIGHT The turquoise waters and steep walls of the Piva canyon in Montenegro. The road, which passes through 56 tunnels in one 25-km (16-mile) stretch, is on the right.
PRECEDING PAGES The Hochstraße (or 'high road'), leading through the Black Forest in Germany.

Having taken refuge under a motorway bridge near Kayseri in Turkey, we wake to the sight of hundreds of sheep filing through the campsite – an unexpected start to the day.

ABOVE While sometimes difficult to find between towns, wild campsites in temperate areas are often very comfortable on account of the vegetation.

RIGHT The predawn light in the highlands of Azerbaijan, before descending down to the Caspian Sea.

OPPOSITE Heading into the town of Tsnori, Georgia, to pick up food and supplies, before finding somewhere to camp.

Squeezing out the last few kilometres from another day on the plains of inland
Turkey, and waiting for the opportune moment to retreat from the road and set up camp.

ABOVE Riding through
the subtropical forests in
Georgia, just inland from the
Black Sea, in early spring.
LEFT An old stone
arch bridge across the
Acharistsqali River in Georgia.
OVERLEAF Just outside
Kastelruth, in the Dolomites:
if the sun is out and the sky is
blue, winter can be a magical
time to ride in the Alps.
ON P. 64 Negotiating snow,
unmade roads, overloaded
vehicles and failing light on the
upper slopes of the Goderdzi
Pass in southern Georgia.

2
DESERTS

AKTAU, KAZAKHSTAN – DUSHANBE, TAJIKISTAN

AKTAU, KAZAKHSTAN–DUSHANBE, TAJIKISTAN

2,000 KM (1,243 MILES), MAY–JUNE

KAZAKHSTAN, UZBEKISTAN

TERRAIN: **DIRT, SAND, TARMAC**

FEATURED BIKE: **FATBIKE**

MOST VALUED ITEM OF KIT: **DROMEDARY WATER BAG**

IT'S HOT.

Not deathly hot, but uncomfortable at the very least. The naked sun, hanging high above in a monotonic blue sky, beats down onto whatever surface breaks its rays, which out here in the Uzbek desert is one of two things: the ground, or us. I go to sit down, but the heat radiating from the sand is too much to bear for more than a few seconds, and I get up again, scanning my surroundings for shelter.

I see Rob standing next to his bike a few hundred metres up the road. He points to a nearby sign. Its paint is peeling, and there are tears of stained rust streaming from the weathered bolts, partially hiding some words in indecipherable Cyrillic script. It's the only object for miles, and we approach it in hope of cover, but the only sanctuary it provides is a 5 cm (2 in.)-wide strip of shade directly beneath it. In a futile attempt to salvage the situation, I erect a tent, but when it's up and I climb inside, the sun seems magnified within its walls, and without the fresh air – if you can call it that – it's even more intolerable than outside.

'What do we have to eat?' I ask Rob.

'Rice. And a stock cube. Oh, we have those instant noodles, too,' he says, rummaging through a pannier. His bike is on its side in the middle of an empty road.

'Do we have enough water to cook them?'

He inspects the contents of the cumbersome plastic bottle we've been carrying. 'Probably not.'

We cook the noodles anyway, giving our bodies the refreshing blast of salt they crave, then slurp the last of the tepid water down, pick up our bikes from the patches of tarmac we threw them down on, and continue riding. Our map says there's a village off the road in about 30 km (19 miles), and we just hope it's right.

· · ·

The desert, as we were discovering, is a rare and unique place to ride through. While its appearance screams openness, it can also feel enclosed; what it lacks in the physical hardships of a long climb, it makes up for in the mental struggle of riding to an ever-distant horizon. The pedals seem to understand the Sisyphean nature of their task. But despite – or because of – the monotony of the rotating pedals and the endless landscape, riding through it yields as much variety of experience as any other environment. If anything, the emptiness only heightens that feeling.

'In the desert I had found a freedom unattainable in civilization; a life unhampered by possessions, since everything that was not a necessity was an encumbrance,' wrote the explorer Wilfred Thesiger in *Arabian Sands* (1959). Huge, empty, without distractions, and forcing our minds to focus on what's important, the simplicity of the desert can be a hugely liberating environment to go cycle touring in, despite the problems its climate presents. The world's desert regions are spread across the seven continents. Heavyweights such as the Sahara in Africa, the Taklamakan in Asia, the Arabian sands in the Middle East or the polar desert regions require an extreme attitude and exhaustive levels of planning before embarking on a cycle tour, but cyclists nonetheless do venture to these remote and inhospitable places. More accessible desert regions include the Mojave in the southwestern United States, the Australian Outback and the Tabernas in Spain, while the Thar in northern India, the Atacama in South America and the Kalahari in southern Africa provide a more exotic – but entirely attainable – experience.

After crossing the Caspian Sea as the only passengers aboard a freight ship filled with frozen chicken legs, our route was set to negotiate the Mangystau and Karakum deserts, in Kazakhstan and Uzbekistan, respectively, which lie between the sea and the mountains further east. The region is a conglomeration of geographic peculiarities: dunes, plateaus, steppes, salt flats and inland seas, stretching out into the heart of Central Asia. But with the Caspian at our backs and looking inland from its eastern shore, the view in front of us was so expansive and desolate that to imagine it changing at some point in the distance was incomprehensible.

Not knowing much about what lay ahead, other than that it would be remote and hot, we set about building as much water-carrying potential into our bikes as we could. In addition to the two bottle cages on my bike, I fixed a third to the top tube with hose clips, used for the first time on the trip, and dusted off a 10-litre (2-gallon) MSR dromedary bag I had been carrying around. Rob was given the unenviable task of transporting a bulky plastic bottle, so between us we had a little over 15 litres (3 gallons) of water when fully stocked. For food, we needed easily transportable, nonperishable calories, so after docking in Aktau we headed to the markets to pick up rice, pasta, noodles and a few onions.

CHOOSING THE RIGHT BIKE:

FATBIKE

The best type of bike for riding in very extreme environments, such as tours that involve off-road desert crossings, unpaved mountain tracks or a lot of snow and ice, is a fatbike. As the name suggests, the oversized ('fat') tyres are their defining feature, but they have their ancestry in mountain bikes and are essentially an unsuspended, beefed-up version. Don't expect to cover many kilometres on a fatbike, but do expect to cover kilometres where few others will be able to follow in your tracks.

1. STEEL FRAME

A steel frame provides comfort and strength, and the extra-wide fork and stay widths allow the oversized wheels to slot in neatly. Some brands include bosses on the fork arms, which can be used for attaching bottle cages or extra luggage.

2. TYRE SIZE

Fatbike tyres are typically 7.5 to 10 cm (3 to 4 in.) wide, on a 26 in., or 66 cm, rim. The volume of air they can hold lets them run with very low pressures, maximizing contact and shock absorption and increasing traction over testing terrain.

3. DISC BRAKES

The de-facto standard for fatbikes, because of the rim size; cantilever options are also available. With the type of riding that fatbikes are associated with, however, the superior braking power of discs will be welcome.

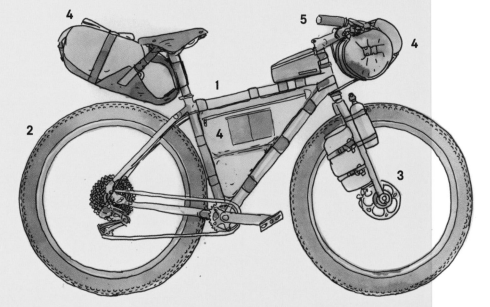

4. LIGHTWEIGHT LUGGAGE

Fatbikes don't leave a lot of room for luggage. To make the most of their benefits (agility, bounciness, handling), keep things light and use a reduced setup of seat pack, frame bag and top-tube bags, and a handlebar bag. Racks are available, but the less you carry, the less you'll have to manoeuvre over tricky terrain.

5. WIDE HANDLEBARS

The laws of physics dictate that wider handlebars give greater steering control, which will be important in extreme riding conditions.

CYCLING IN
HOT WEATHER

Attach multiple bottle cages to your frame. Some frames come with extra mounts on the underside of the down tube; using hose clips to attach them is another option.

Get a dromedary bag: they're easily portable and can hold a lot of fluid.

Plan appropriately. Hot and remote environments are the sort of places where the consequences could be worse than normal. Do you know where to find food and water? Do you know where people are likely to be found?

If going off-road, ensure you're familiar with maps of the local area and, if you're taking one, that your GPS is reliable and charged.

Cover up, even though it's hot. Applying sun cream isn't going to hurt either. When the sun is out, you'll need to be protected.

SPD sandals: your feet can get smelly and uncomfortable when confined to a pair of shoes in the heat. Shimano and other brands offer sandals with SPD pedal fittings, which can be a good option.

Snakes, scorpions and other nasty creatures lurk in the desert, so check your campsite for any strange-looking holes before pitching, and double-check clothes, shoes and sleeping bags before getting into them.

Tent pegs don't stay put in the sand. Make sure your tent is self-supported, or try to find long sticks to use as stakes.

Don't forget to eat. A loss of appetite is common in the heat, but if you're planning on cycling every day, you will need the calories.

Take a siesta: if it's too hot to ride during the day, don't do it. Get up early and get your kilometres in before lunch, and then find somewhere sheltered to rest during the afternoon.

Even in the desert, overnight temperatures can drop to well below what they were during the day, so make sure you've got the right sleeping bag and clothes.

Bring products to clean your chain. The sand and dust will stick to it and become a grinding paste, destroying the entire drivetrain system. Degrease (you can use fuel from the stove in an emergency), clean and re-lube your chain regularly.

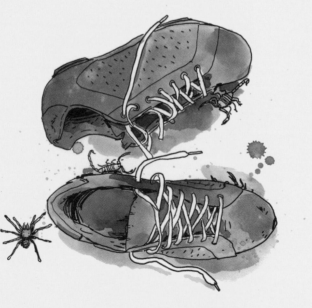

We had bought enough stock cubes to supply a small army, as well as some packets of dried herbs and a smattering of salt, just for a little pizzazz. Needing to make room for the extra supplies, and to remain as agile as possible in this unforgiving environment, we stripped ourselves and our bikes of anything superfluous. Layers of winter clothing, old maps and non-essentials like playing cards and some camera paraphernalia were discarded or mailed home.

When entering a region you know little or nothing about, especially one as potentially hazardous as the desert, doing some research ahead of time is essential. Even if our map didn't give much away, Google's satellite feature seemed to show a few, very minor settlements along the road, which we marked on our map as best we could. We stayed with an unlikely local American resident to seek advice – 'There's really not much out there,' he had said with a chuckle – and found dated journals from previous cyclists on Crazyguyonabike.com (see p. 258), which alerted us to potential sanctuaries along the way. Rarely did our estimates prove to be correct, but the hope they provided was invaluable as we began to get a thirst or hunger on. 'Only another twenty kilometres until the next stop, we'll be there soon,' we would tell ourselves, and find the motivation to keep grinding away.

At first, tabletop rock formations appeared intermittently at the sides of the road, graded with horizontal bands of colour and puncturing the otherwise flat skyline, adding to the unearthly nature of the desert. Occasionally, a watering hole would shimmer into view, with its entourage of wild horses, camels, even the odd flamingo, but after 200 km (124 miles) or so, the road finally climbed up onto the Ustyurt plateau, and the meagre roadside entertainment disappeared. So flat and featureless was the landscape that perceptions of scale and distance were impossible to gauge. The same mixture of sand and grass spilling over into the road next to us simply continued to its own featureless horizon, which could have been 30 kilometres away or three. Had we been on fatbikes or mountain bikes, venturing off-road and into the depths of the interior to go in search of even remoter parts would have been very tempting, but with our fully loaded expedition bikes we were confined to the main carriageway.

For a while a lonely railway line ran parallel to the road, providing a small indication of scale – which, considering that the pylons merely disappeared, arrow-straight, into nothing, wasn't necessarily appreciated. The only other signs of life were tyre tracks that occasionally veered off into the abyss; a few shepherds, often mounted and protected from the sun with full-face balaclavas; or the clustered minarets of deserted burial grounds, lying dormant in a patch of distant sand. But the rumbling sound of a passing train in the night or a brief exchange with a full-time resident of such a hostile environment provided a certain amount of comfort in a place where it was otherwise absent.

Our biggest reprieve, offering mental stimulation and physical rest, were the *chaihanas* that appeared every 60 to 100 km (37 to 62 miles) or so, an indent of variation on the horizon that prompted a nod of appreciative understanding between us, followed by what felt like an achingly long ride towards it. These roadside tea houses are among the most instantly recognizable features throughout Central Asia, and their unkempt appearance, basic services and limited menus of just one or two regional dishes – which in Central Asia was *plov* (rice), *manti* (dumplings) or *lagman* (noodles) – provided a rare constant on the road.

These low-key establishments provided shelter from the sun and relentless wind, and a safe environment in which we could stop for an hour or so to eat, drink and take a break from the elements. A *chaihana*'s fundamental purpose is to serve tea and a basic meal, but many also provide some sort of primitive sleeping arrangement for a travelling clientele of truck drivers, tradesmen and adventure cyclists. Those in settlements are often also a place of social interaction for locals. The way they

NAVIGATION

Navigation skills are essential to any bike tour, regardless of length, climate or terrain. There are three main aids to help you navigate effectively: paper maps, GPS devices and asking a local for directions. It is often best to use a combination of all three.

PAPER MAPS

Poring over a crumpled paper map by a campfire, planning the next day's itinerary, is an essential element of cycle touring. Paper maps are a good way to get an overview of the lay of the land and are also relatively cheap and disposable, so they can be traded (along with advice) with travellers met coming the other way.

GPS DEVICES

GPS devices, or smartphones with GPS, are useful in remote areas and in cities, when following a pre-planned route where keeping on track is essential. Using digitized onscreen maps and accurate pinpointing, you can upload GPX files or work out a direction from your position on the inbuilt map.

LOCAL KNOWLEDGE

Asking for advice can reveal alternative routes, unknown scenic locations or the presence of a service off the main road you may find yourself needing. Be wary of presenting a map to people, as they may never have seen one before, let alone know how to read it, but this will not stop them giving you spurious directions anyway. It's also worth noting that directions from people who don't drive, ride a bicycle or rarely leave their own village must be taken with a pinch of salt.

LANGUAGE

Bike-touring in foreign countries will more often than not mean immersing yourself in a place where people speak a different language. Communicating, or attempting to, in the local language will be appreciated, but be clever about the languages you invest time in learning, especially if there is a lingua franca in the different countries you are visiting. English is a good place to start anywhere in the world, but you might consider brushing up on your Spanish for a tour in Latin America, Russian for any ex-Soviet states, French for central and western Africa, or Arabic for north Africa and the Middle East.

A single word will often be enough for people to put the rest of the sentence together and work out what you're trying to say. Here are some essentials that will come in handy:

The basics ('hello', 'goodbye', 'thank you')

'Bicycle'

'Which way to [...]?', or just naming the place you want to get – which usually has the same effect.

'Possible?', together with a well-acted pantomime, can mean any of the following: 'Can I buy these?'; 'Is this road passable?'; 'Is my bike broken?'; 'Will it rain?'; 'Will you settle for that price?'

'Good!' or 'great!'. Use often, they will earn you friends.

'How are you?' Same as above, even though you may not understand the response.

Your nationality, age and marital status: you'll be asked this, a lot.

How many kilometres you've ridden: you'll be asked this, a lot.

Amenities (restaurant, hotel, bike shop, doctor).

Food (bread, rice, water, meat, vegetables, tea).

broke the monotony of the desert, enabled contact and conversation with the locals and offered the security of bricks and mortar also added a morale-boosting dimension to these modest buildings.

The Uzbek border, when it eventually materialized, was like a pinprick of life that had somehow managed to escape the desolation around it. It was an unexpected hive of activity, with encampments of people sheltering from the sun beneath sheets of tarpaulin and snoozing with their backs against their luggage as they passed the time and waited to be filed through. Once at the front of the queue, customs proved to be scrupulous, with a complete overhaul of our bikes and gear performed in front of curious onlookers. We'd read that there were only two ATMs in the entire country, so we worked out a budget for our stay and exchanged some of the American dollars we'd withdrawn in Baku with the black-market operatives at the border. In some parts of the world it is quite common, even if people have heard of the pound, Euro or other currencies, not to accept them in exchange, and so it often pays – literally – to keep a stash of US dollars, and top it up at every available opportunity. Denominations of less than $10 are generally not accepted, and in some places (Myanmar, from experience), only the cleanest, crispest, newest $100 bills can be exchanged.

Once into Uzbekistan we found ourselves sandwiched between the Kyzylkum and Karakum deserts. Rolling dunes lined the roadside, until replaced by the cracked, muddy jigsaws of long-parched bodies of water. The road frequently dissolved into myriad dirt tracks, corrugated and compacted by lorries, which widened as drivers searched for smooth ground on either side. While in some ways tiresome, the distraction that a poorly surfaced road offered, forcing us to thread our front wheels around potholes and patches of sand in search of a clear line, was a welcome break from the mind-numbing blankness. It provided a challenge to get our teeth into, and helped us forget the niggling pains and boredom brought on by riding in a straight line, kilometre after kilometre.

The temperature rose as we moved further south, forcing us to buy sandals to relieve our throbbing, smelly feet, and burning our backs into a mess of blisters, even through shirts and sunscreen. The ancient Silk Road settlements of Khiva, Bukhara and Samarkand provided a romantic portal into the region's historic past, as well as the opportunity to fix our bikes, repair broken equipment and allow ourselves some rest, before embarking on the next stretch of desert. (See pp. 217–32 for more about the benefits of cities.)

Our final night in the desert came after a long, 190-km (118-mile) day. It had gone 8 o'clock, the sun had already dipped below the horizon, and the two pedalling shadows we had cast on the sand had finally disappeared. We were hot, sticky and tired after 10 hours of riding when we noticed three yurts between the sand and shrubbery. In need of water, and preferring that the inhabitants were aware of our presence, rather than stumbling upon us during the night, we approached and chatted in broken Russian about our trip and their 1,000-strong herd of sheep, before asking if we could camp in the vicinity. 'Nyeh prablema,' was the reply. We set about hoisting our tents, surrounded by our inquisitive hosts and their excitable children, but it wasn't long before we were stopped and told they wouldn't be necessary.

After cooking some food, and causing much amusement with our petrol stove, flint-sparking stick and dromedary water sack, we were invited into the cosy surroundings of one of the yurts. Some people were already in bed, so it was hard to tell who we had for company (although at least three generations seemed to be represented), and we were shown to two spaces among the eight or so bodies in which to curl up. The men went about their tasks, before the last person silently turned off the oil lamp and tiptoed his way to bed. The door was kept open all night, and one roll of the animal hides that formed the outer wall was also pulled up, leaving a panoramic view out across the peaceful, still desert. The breeze was cool, the sky was clear, and the sound of one final hushed conversation between our hosts sent me off to sleep.

Rob and I then split up for the first time since meeting in Istanbul, as I raced on ahead to get to Dushanbe in Tajikistan and begin the process of my Indian visa application. Our Tajik visas were due to start imminently, and the more time we spent in Uzbekistan, the more we'd eat into our allotted 30-day stay. I did not want to waste it by waiting around for the time-consuming process of visa applications.

As I rolled into the golden hills that rise in the far south of Uzbekistan, I encountered the first slopes of a chain of mountain ranges that includes the highest of them all, the Himalaya. But India, where I would later experience this mighty mountain system to the full, felt so far away that it could almost be part of another world, and if it wasn't for the knowledge that the southern edge of the mountains ahead fell on Indian soil, it may as well have been. As we continued to learn, despite the huge distances, international border crossings and disparities in environment, the world of the cycle tourist is often a microcosm in itself.

The immediate concerns of food, water and where to sleep were always at the forefront, cultivating a routine that could be adapted to suit any obstacles and environments encountered. With little to distract our attention, the emptiness of the desert and our unchanging routine made us aware of how attuned and practised we were as cycle tourists, from packing a pannier and unfurling a tent to the shared recognition of when it was time to stop or to go, when someone needed to be avoided or when a stray dog was about to start a charge for one's leg.

Like an artist's blank canvas, the emptiness of the desert provides the potential for such freedom. But because of its extreme, unmerciful climate, there is also restriction in its openness. As Thesiger noted in *Arabian Sands*, the desert's freedom, while outwardly hostile and prohibitive, is manifested in the way it allows both a disconnect from the superfluous and a purity of day-to-day

EATING
ON THE
ROAD

With the amount of calories burned, eating well on a bike tour is essential. What exactly a rider will eat, however, will largely depend on the tour itself.

Many cyclists choose to travel with a camping stove [see p. 181], a tool that enables a certain degree of self-sufficiency when preparing meals. For short trips, these stoves might be used just to boil water to add to a dehydrated food pouch; on longer ones, they can be used to cook a hearty meal, whether on the pavement outside of a supermarket or at a wild campsite in the middle of nowhere.

The length and intensity of the trip will also decide how food is sourced. Some may choose to bring a supply of foodstuffs from home, but most riders will have packed their stoves with the knowledge that food will need to be sourced on the road. When cooking yourself, make sure you follow the normal advice and keep your diet as balanced as you can. You'll need carbohydrates for energy, protein for recovery and vitamins from fruit and vegetables to stave off sickness – even more than usual, so try to get them in wherever possible.

In much of the world, buying food could not be easier, but outside of developed countries it can often be difficult to find any kind of 'food' shops at all. Small-scale eateries can usually be found, but owing to the self-sufficiency of local residents, it can be difficult to buy unprepared, storable food to cook yourself.

Luckily, in much of the world it is often cheaper, easier and tastier to dine at the local eateries, so be sure to take advantage of the local cuisine. There will generally be a local dish, served ubiquitously in restaurants, which is designed to tick all of the nutritional boxes at a price people can afford. With the help of a plastic container, reheating restaurant-bought dishes like these at a campsite later on in the day is also an option. **For many cyclists travelling in remote areas, where self-sufficiency is essential, the most popular energy-giving foodstuffs are rice and instant noodles, with some flavour added from a modest on-bike larder (salt, pepper, stock) and supplemented with whatever else can be found.**

CYCLING
IN REMOTE
PLACES

There is no doubt that cycling in remote regions offers an experience that most cycle tourists crave, as it is in the deserts, mountains and jungles that nature is at its most spectacular and extreme, and civilization is at its most bare.

As a result, these places are where the travelling cyclist often feels most at home. But it is what attracts us that also makes them places to be treated with caution, respect and a little more forethought than more-populated areas. It is useful to keep these tips in mind when venturing into the more remote reaches of the globe:

Get to know an area as much as possible beforehand, building up a picture of what might lay ahead.

Try to source maps where possible, and remember that this can sometimes be easier at home than in a foreign country.

In the absence of a map, draw your own with pen and paper from advice and guidance sought out locally or from other travellers.

Make notes of where you will be most likely to find water sources, food and other people. Mark them on a map if possible.

In the absence of a map, make notes of landmarks, villages, or other distinguishing features to navigate and keep track of progress.

Consider using a GPS device for precise navigation, or bringing a device such as a Spot Tracker in order to send out an automatic SOS signal, should the need arise.

In case of emergencies, always be aware of where the next nearest person is likely to be found. Will they be in a shepherd's hut over the next hill, passing by in a car every few hours, or in a town 200 km (124 miles) away? Prevention is always better than cure. Try to stay hydrated and nourished, be wary of alcohol and other intoxicants, and get as much rest as possible. **Be pessimistic with times and distances. Assume that a stretch that should take two days to complete will take three, and pack food supplies accordingly.** Think about space-weight-necessity ratios when packing. Travelling light keeps you nimble, but in remote regions there is a lot more luggage required for self-sufficiency.

Make sure you know how to fix everything that could go wrong with your bike. Before entering a remote region, notify someone (who you are in regular contact with) of your plans, and when to expect to hear from you again.

existence: 'Everything that was not a necessity was an encumbrance.'

Our world was a self-sufficient, unencumbered bubble of routine and security that we rode inside, from one day to the next, through awe-inspiring landscapes, ancient cities and remote towns, across boundaries of nation, ethnicity, language and terrain. We cycled and lived them all. And like the act of riding a bicycle, the unforgiving climes of the desert and the pains of bureaucracy dictated that to keep our balance, we had to keep moving forward.

A rare sighting of a car, emerging from the dust. Be prepared
to stop any vehicles that appear for water or advice, if necessary.

ABOVE Rock formations can sometimes feel like the only way to gauge progress.

RIGHT Rob in his tent, enjoying the sun's last rays and the silence of the desert.

OVERLEAF Making the most of the straight, flat roads in Kazakhstan, and putting the hammer down for some big-kilometre days. Note the burial ground in the distance.

ON P. 81 Clever packing is essential in remote regions, as is bike choice: we found our road tourers a little under-equipped for off-piste adventuring.

ABOVE Rob rides through dust kicked up by a long-departed vehicle.
RIGHT Stray dogs are a regular sight. This one followed us for over 10 km (6 miles).
OPPOSITE Making dinner amid the bikes, bags and tents cluttering an otherwise deserted patch of sand (above). Stopping to investigate the animals drinking water at the side of the road (below).
OVERLEAF A lunch of instant noodles in Uzbekistan, concocted in minutes.

ABOVE Collecting much-needed water from a well at the back of a *chaihana*.
RIGHT A 'ship graveyard' at what was the fishing port of Moynaq, Uzbekistan, now almost 300 km (186 miles) from the Aral Sea.
LEFT The barren flatlands and curious rock formations of the Mangystau region in Kazakhstan.
OVERLEAF A 5am glow warms the eastern flank of the shepherd's yurt we took shelter in, somewhere between Urgench and Bukhara in Uzbekistan.

ABOVE Fighting off the morning chill in the desert.
LEFT Entertaining the local children with our 'velocipedy' (bicycles).
RIGHT Pushing back to the road through the sand after departing the yurt site.
OVERLEAF Dramatic skies bring the day to a close in the Kyzylkum desert, Uzbekistan.

RIGHT A reminder to be wary of the local wildlife when venturing into foreign lands.
BELOW Unzipping the tent to survey the morning camp scene. Mostly it would be exactly as you left it.
OPPOSITE The Ustyurt plateau in Kazakhstan. Its sheer emptiness was overwhelming at times.
OVERLEAF The joy of riding at dusk can make the necessity of stopping to find a campsite hard to face up to.

ABOVE The road to the Uzbek border from Beyneu, Kazakhstan, frequented by cyclists and HGVs alike.
RIGHT The modest (and in this case, quite presentable) interior of a *chaihana*, a welcome sanctuary of food, water and shelter in the desert.
LEFT Combating the boredom of having nothing to look at by taking self-timed photos.
ON P. 104 A roaming donkey decides to investigate the middle of the road in Uzbekistan.

3

MOUNTAINS

DUSHANBE, TAJIKISTAN–SHIMLA, INDIA

4,500 KM (2,796 MILES), JUNE–SEPTEMBER

TAJIKISTAN, KYRGYZSTAN, CHINA, PAKISTAN, INDIA

TERRAIN: **GRAVEL, ROCK-HEWN, SANDY, TARMAC**

FEATURED BIKE: **MOUNTAIN BIKE**

MOST VALUED ITEM OF KIT: **CAMERA**

I LOOK DOWN AT MY SPEEDOMETER

and squint dejectedly at the number displayed –
a measly 3 kph (1.8 mph). My eyes are drawn beyond
the speedo to the ground below, a punishing mixture
of sand and rock, with the fresh tyre tracks of my com-
panions weaving drunkenly through them. Then I look
up again, noticing a blanket of looming black clouds,
and lose my balance, forcing me to put my foot down
and slump wearily over the handlebars.

Progress is glacially slow, but at these altitudes it is
a speed that must be accepted. The threat posed by the
impending snowstorm means we need to get over and
off the mountain as quickly as possible, but difficulty
in breathing and the abominable road surface mean
there is no possibility of speeding things up. Riding
hard is impossible: I am barely able to consume enough

oxygen to sustain aerobic efforts, let alone anaerobic, so must be patient with the smallest gear I have, and drag myself to the top at whichever slow speed it carries me – even if it is 3 kph.

I get going again, and for a few minutes the rhythmic passing of time is consuming enough to allow me to forget about the summit for a while. At 4,344 m (14,250 ft) it will be the highest of the journey so far, and one of a series in excess of 4,000 m (13,120 ft) along the Pamir Highway. A glance at my watch reveals the time to be 4:30pm. With the light now beginning to fade, it feels as if there's a long way to go before I can call it a day. I just hope that the snow, when it does begin to fall, doesn't last for long.

• • •

The hostility of mountain terrain makes travel inherently problematic and physically challenging, especially on a bicycle. But therein lies its beauty for adventure cyclists, with its confluence of agony and ecstasy, and the effort required repaid by breathtaking views and rich cultural variation. For cyclists and travellers, there is no better place to satisfy our natural thirst for adventure and beauty. My onward route through Tajikistan, Kyrgyzstan, China, Pakistan and India would eventually leave me with over 4,000 km (2,500 miles) of some of the world's most distinguishable mountain landscape beneath my wheels.

The Alps had provided my first encounter with mountains proper back in January. The fluctuations of a mountain climate need no reiteration here, and being out of season, in the midst of a European winter, meant that my experiences had been entirely governed by the weather. On numerous occasions I was forced to take refuge for days on end, waiting for passes to open or roads to be ploughed, but when the weather did clear, I was rewarded with smooth tarmac, blue skies and low winter sun, dazzling against the snowy peaks.

Once on the passes, I found myself in the company of skiers and snowboarders. In the summer these Alpine climbs, immortalized by their appearances in the Tour de France and the Giro d'Italia, are crawling with cyclists, drawn by good tarmac roads, an abundance of hotels and the comforts of Europe, picture-postcard vistas and sporting heritage. Their pilgrimages, I could see, were truly justified. But my Lycra-clad presence up there during the winter months was not expected, and caused some jovial confusion among the tourists: 'Du bist kalt, nein?'

If the Alps was a sea of great whites, then the smaller Balkan ranges that followed had been an ocean of piranhas, nibbling away at my strength with their incessant sharp inclines. The mountains of Turkey and the Caucasus were like a bridge between Europe and Asia, both physically – being bigger, higher and more expansive – and in the way that life there was wilder and more raw compared to Europe, bearing witness to the dramatic, intercontinental shifts in the ethnicity and culture of the inhabitants.

Cycling out of Dushanbe, the capital of Tajikistan, into the western edge of the Pamirs should have been a moment to savour. Unfortunately, as can often happen on such long trips, my Indian visa application had been delayed and then denied by the consul in Dushanbe. On top of this, my body was suffering from yet another bout of food poisoning – a familiar hazard on such expeditions.

Rob and Pete, who had flown out to meet me, had left a couple of days earlier, so I was riding hard and alone to catch up. My body was ejecting fluids in any way it could, and a total loss of appetite meant that I was cycling on the calorific yield of a few measly mouthfuls of rice. Collapsed in my tent in a feverish state wasn't the way I had intended to embark on my journey to the 'Roof of the World', but these are the cards that adventure cyclists are dealt from time to time. Nonetheless, I was filled with anticipation.

CHOOSING THE RIGHT BIKE:

MOUNTAIN

Mountain bikes first appeared in the 1970s, dramatically expanding the type of terrain that could be explored by bicycle. Their fundamental characteristics haven't aged a bit since. Not quite as extreme as a fatbike (see pp. 68–9), but still very much optimized for off-road riding, mountain bikes are a great choice for tours where the majority of the route is unpaved, and where even a chunky-tyred touring bike won't do.

1. FAT TYRES

The bigger the tyre, the more surface area will be in contact with the ground, thus affording more traction and grip. Lowering pressures in the tyres has the same effect.

2. WHEEL SIZE

Wheels are traditionally 26-in., manoeuvrable and freely available worldwide. A more contemporary choice is the 29-in. wheel, which offers better rolling capabilities.

3. LUGGAGE

Slimline bikepacking bags are perfect for the type of riding that mountain bikes are used for, where manoeuvrability and handling are key.

4. MECHANICAL DISC BRAKES

Mountain-bike terrain requires a lot of braking. Disc brakes perform better and are more hardwearing than rim brakes. Avoid hydraulic systems in case of rupture in remote areas.

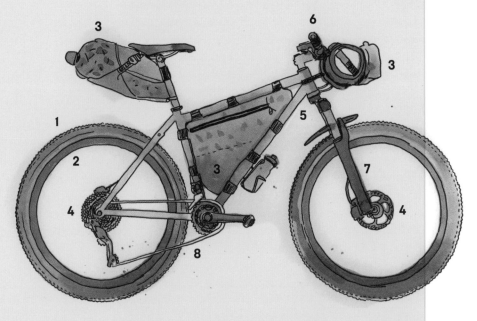

5. STABLE GEOMETRY

Slack head tube and seat tube angles, a longer wheelbase and lengthy chainstays give mountain bikes their stability.

6. WIDE HANDLEBARS

More width means greater sensitivity in handling, which is useful for navigating the best line through unmade tracks.

7. SUSPENSION

Rigid or hard-tail frames are both fine, while full-suspension mountain bikes are impractical for touring purposes.

8. SMALL GEAR RATIOS

Mountain bikes come with smaller gears as standard, making climbs as easy as possible.

DEALING WITH ALTITUDE SICKNESS

If you're venturing into regions above 2,000 m (6,500 ft), the chances are you will feel at least some of the effects of altitude sickness. The symptoms can be as minimal as a slight headache, but in its extreme stages altitude sickness can be fatal, and must always be respected.

Make a gradual ascent: allowing your body time to adapt is a crucial part of any mountain activity, and adventure cycling is no different.

Do as the mountaineers do: climb high, sleep low. If you've got a particularly high pass to tackle, don't sleep on the summit – try to get over it and find some lower ground.

Take note of breathing patterns and general wellbeing. Are you waking up short of breath? Having difficulties catching your breath?

Unable to breathe deeply? Suffering from headaches and nausea? Some of the above is natural, but if you're concerned, don't proceed higher until you acclimatize. If symptoms increase, go back down. Keep well hydrated. **Avoid alcohol and smoking.** Speak to a doctor about preventative medications.

When Marco Polo crossed the Pamirs in the 13th century, he noted: 'You get to such a height that it is said to be the highest place in the world! ... You ride across it for twelve days, finding nothing but a desert without habitations or any green thing, so that travellers are obliged to carry with them whatever they have need of.'

No doubt this reflects something of what can be found in other high-altitude regions, such as the Altiplano in South America, a popular touring destination, or Tibet, the largest high-altitude plateau in the world and closed to independent travel since 2008. These regions are distinctly beautiful, presenting mindbendingly huge and near-deserted expanses of arid plains and shallow mountains. The landscape folds and wraps around itself, its empty spaces reflecting the shadows of localized weather systems as if they were projected onto a canvas.

The altitude and lack of oxygen manifests itself in different ways. Difficulties encountered while breathing vary from being unable to push hard on the bike to waking up during the night, gasping for breath, or becoming short of breath while speaking. The stove takes a noticeably long time to boil water and uses up fuel at a far greater rate. Over time, your body and mind become more fatigued than normal and you become more irritable and mentally slower.

Life above a certain altitude is harsh, but with its empty, windswept valleys and peaks, whose gradual slopes and stingy dusting of snow belie their height, the Pamirs are a mountain range of desolate grandeur – a truly vast and unnerving place, well worthy of the title 'Roof of the World'.

Any tour of considerable length will inevitably result in periods of stagnancy, with the wheels forced to stop rolling for one reason or another, whether because of mechanical issues, travel permits, illness or sheer exhaustion. Upon arrival in Bishkek, the capital of Kyrgyzstan, I fell victim to a selection of these. Rob's journey had come to an end, but onward travel for Pete and I into Pakistan required sending our passports back

MAINTENANCE

Unless you're only heading out for a day or two, the chances are you're going to need to fiddle with something on your bike at some point. At the very least, you should have ridden the bike once or twice before embarking on an adventure where you will be completely reliant on it, just to make sure it won't fall apart. Once on the road you could find yourself making repairs anywhere, from a dusty kerb to a hotel forecoUurt, and it pays to be clued up on the basics to ensure this time is kept to a minimum. Make sure you're familiar with:

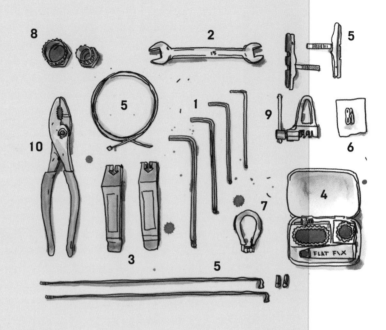

Fixing a puncture and replacing a tyre
Replacing brake pads
Replacing cables (brake and gear)
Adjusting and replacing a derailleur (front and rear)
Removing and installing pedals
Replacing a chain
Tightening a headset
Replacing a broken spoke
Truing a wheel

The need to cover every eventuality usually isn't necessary, and probably isn't even possible. You're hardly likely to carry a spare frame, after all. Spare tyres, spare derailleurs, even spare wheels have been known to go on trips with cyclists, but most full toolkits will have enough to carry out the above tasks. Yours should at least include:

1. **Allen keys / torx wrenches**
2. 15 mm (pedal) spanner
3. **Tyre levers**
4. Puncture-repair kit and patches
5. **Spares for cables, brake pads, spokes**
6. Chain quick link
7. **Spoke keys**
8. Cassette removal tool
9. **Chain breaker**
10. Pliers

For cyclists on longer tours, duct tape and cable ties are invaluable for providing temporary fixes until replacement parts can be sourced.

to London for visas, and we couldn't leave until they were returned. I also had a host of mechanical problems to rectify, which required the sourcing and posting of new parts, so I busied myself with seeing to these, getting my diaries up to date and gathering information about the road ahead, both online and from travellers going the other way.

The journey so far had left me fit, lean and strong, my bike an extension of myself as it rolled beneath me. Cycling at altitude adapts the body to the point where breathing oxygen at more reasonable heights feels like cheating, and my legs were now reaping those benefits. Hygiene offences I had committed, and the culinary ways of the countries I had passed through, had ensured that my immune system was able to fight off the vilest of bugs. My hair was long and, much to the interest of the locals we met along the way, my face was sporting a full red beard. But – as all travellers discover during such endeavours – the head on which the beard grew had become weary.

After six months of continual travel, and with half of my intended journey still ahead of me, I came to the unsettling yet exhilarating realization that cycle touring had effectively become my life. I had passed the point of simply being on 'a trip'. Memories from the beginning of my journey felt distant, and ideas about what lay ahead felt equally disconnected. The mental investment required simply to make it through the hours between waking and falling asleep had almost overridden my ability to take pleasure in the adventure, despite my body being so physically attuned to the demands placed on it.

While we waited for our passports, Pete and I set off on a mini-tour of the country. The nomadic DNA that runs through the Kyrgyz was fascinating to witness, as my own life on a bike gave a certain insight into aspects of theirs, from the placement of yurt camps, in sheltered valleys and always near running water, to the importance of horses (or bikes, in our case).

Kyrgyzstan has a reputation of being the most beautiful country nobody has ever heard of. Being almost entirely mountainous, with a diversity of geography that would usually be enough for an entire continent, it provided the perfect environment in which to rediscover the beauty of adventure cycling and regain excitement for the road ahead.

If Kyrgyzstan had been diverse in terms of landscape, geology and terrain, the mountains we saw while heading south through China's Xinjiang province towards Pakistan offered a diverse spectrum of human geography, caused by the physical divisions they create between communities. We headed onto the Karakoram Highway, a road of cycle-touring legend running between Kashgar and Islamabad, an area that encompasses a substantial amount of racial and cultural diversity. The heritage of the people who watched us as we cycled past was often clearly identifiable from the language they spoke, the clothes they wore or the complexion of their faces. Many probably wouldn't describe themselves as 'Chinese' or 'Pakistani', even though the modern map of the world forces them into one category or the other. This idea of identity transcending manmade borders is typical of the mountain environment.

In the Balkans, much earlier in the trip, the web of ethnicities had proved as difficult to untangle as its mountain passes had been to climb. Country A could lead to country B in name alone, and although my passport doesn't carry a Serbian border stamp (for riding into Bosnia's Republika Srpska out of Sarajevo, for example), I feel as if it should. In the mountainous province of Yunnan, in southern China, it would not be until I had been in the country for 1,000 km (620 miles) that I began to feel the Laotian and Vietnamese influences around its southern border diminish.

The inhabitants of villages that are separated by only a few kilometres, but also by an insurmountable 8,000 m (26,250 ft) wall of rock, or a mountain pass that has only recently been constructed, may speak different

CYCLING
OFF-ROAD

The mountains are usually where you're most likely to encounter the worst roads – and sometimes there may not even be a road. You'll likely find yourself pushing, pulling, dragging and kicking your bike as much as you will riding it, but there are some measures you can take to keep such struggles to a minimum:

Bring the right bike – this isn't the place for a drop-handlebar road bike. The wider the tyres, the better it is for maximum surface area and traction. Let some pressure out of the tyres – another step towards maximizing grip. Wide handlebars mean more width to the steering platform, which in turn gives greater control.

Higher handlebars and a lower saddle give more stability.
Granny ring – the tinier and easier to pedal, the better.
Pannier balancing (see below): distribute weight evenly to ensure the bike is balanced when riding on uneven roads.
If you're only using one set of panniers, put them

at the front to push more weight onto the front wheel, planting it firmly for inclines and into loose dirt.
Travelling light gives you more manoeuvrability – and less weight to carry. Pack everything tightly to make sure nothing bounces off in the rough stuff.
Check bolts regularly – lots of jolting can cause them to start to loosen. Be wary of clipless pedals and straps, as there will be plenty of occasions when you need to put your foot down on the road. Pressure control, or subtly adjusting the weight applied to the bike by the way you hold yourself on it, is an expert skill that is invaluable when descending over ground strewn with large obstacles.

STAYING SAFE
ON THE ROAD

Staying safe on a tour of any length is something most people would agree is important. Others (insurance providers and mums included) might claim that by its very nature adventure cycling is unsafe: going to places you've never been before, where you won't speak the language, with only a bicycle for security. Sounds risky, right? Wrong. In the experience of adventure cyclists around the world, these are the aspects of cycle-touring life that often ensure your safety. Whether you like it or not, many will see you as someone in need of assistance and protection, either because of concern for your wellbeing or a wider cultural belief. It can be a tricky situation to come to terms with, as much of the time you will find that these well-meaning people will be financially far worse off than you, so make sure you are aware of what's expected of you as a guest. In some parts of the world you pay for the help you receive simply by accepting it; in others you might be expected to offer a gift or – surprise, surprise – money. But dealing extravagant hospitality is part and parcel of cycle touring, and is why you needn't fear for your safety. Friendliness isn't always unconditional, however, and you could encounter some difficult situations and shady characters you'll have to deal with. They usually aren't a problem unless you allow them to become one, so if you feel the tone taking a downward turn, just be aware of it. Don't be confrontational: if there's alcohol involved, try and steer clear of it; don't go flashing things like cash or cameras around, and do your best to diffuse the situation. Smile, shake hands, start talking about football and showering people with compliments ('Lionel Messi is a fantastic player'; 'Your country is so beautiful!') You will be amazed at how quickly it gets the drunk official trying to get a bribe out of you off of your back. That's the important stuff dealt with. Now here are some practical tips:

Don't ride if you're in really bad health
Ride in a visible but conservative road position
Try to avoid highways wherever possible
Use lights and high-vis clothing if riding in bad visibility or at night
Don't ride aggressively
Don't descend faster than is sensible
Avoid the stress and think about catching a train into a major city
And lastly, protect your head with a helmet when necessary

Take a bike lock
Don't leave your bike unattended without the help of an impromptu guard (riding partner, shopkeeper or hotel receptionist). **Leave your bike near your tent at night or bring it into your hotel room.**

Try not to carry large amounts of cash, and distribute what you do have around your luggage. **Keep important documents close to hand at all times (in a detachable handlebar bag, for example).**

languages, worship different gods and trace their racial heritage to more distant lands, but both are ultimately still looking up at the same peak. The impenetrable, timeless force of a mountain range can never be truly tamed by lines drawn in the sand, demarcating one place from the next, and for that reason there is a palpable universality shared across these regions. The mountains divide, but also unite, and in no way is this more perceptible than if you make your way slowly overland between them, one pedal rev at a time.

As my route progressed east, the mountains I encountered had formed an evolving narrative. The Alps, despite crossing in winter, had played an introductory note, while the Balkans and Caucasus had proved more testing and foreign, on a variety of levels. The Pamirs had represented something of an endurance test, with their remoteness and high altitudes demanding that I call upon all I had learned about cycle touring up to that point, and the mountains of Kyrgyzstan had given fresh breath to the exhausted state in which they had left me.

Pakistan and India, where this mountain narrative continued, lie at the very heart of the Asian mountain system, and the character of their ranges – particularly the Karakoram and Himalaya – also gave a new perspective on cycle touring in the mountains. Like relationships with people, music or art, there is a duality in the emotional connection we have with them that is perhaps best represented by these, the world's tallest ranges, which appear both celestial and intimidating to the cyclist riding beneath them.

We had gone to great lengths to obtain a visa for Pakistan, and as a result Pete and I are among a lucky handful to have cycled across Eurasia by connecting the northern and southern routes, to which the Karakoram Highway, and Pakistan's high international border with China, holds the key. With its preliminary paperwork, social stigma and a good deal of the unknown and un-researchable, entry and overland travel through Pakistan had in many ways been the biggest obstacle

ELECTRONICS: WHAT TO BRING AND HOW TO CHARGE THEM

While getting out and exploring the world by bike is about getting back to nature and cutting off ties with the plugged-in world, there are few people who will ride off without carrying at least one or two electronic devices.

Mobile phones, which most people will have at the very least, can be used almost anywhere in the world, providing they have a compatible SIM card. Smartphones can double up as a camera, navigation device, web browser, and more.

Digital cameras are light, compact and easy to transport, but once you start moving into DSLR territory, you must think carefully about the practicalities of carrying it and charging the batteries.

If you're planning a long-distance tour and need the extra data storage and web-browsing benefits of a laptop, make sure you keep it in a relatively dry environment, protected from jolts, when loaded on the bike.

GPS devices are a commonly used and sometimes essential bit of gear for routes that veer into expedition territory, with off-road and unexplored areas where getting lost can have serious consequences. As they are also useful for simply keeping track of distance and location, as well as pinpointing locations in urban areas, there is a lot to be said for taking a GPS.

Other items in an adventure cyclist's electrical arsenal include lights (torch, head torch, bike lights), an FM radio and a satellite tracker (a basic tracking device that sends your location to pre-assigned recipients at the push of a button), all of which are usually battery-powered (AA/AAA) or USB-rechargeable.

Unless you're going super-off-piste, you will likely find a place to charge your most important electricals every few days or so. Take extra batteries for items like DSLR cameras and lights, but if you're using a laptop when out in the wilds then, frankly, you'd better hope it dies so that you can start paying attention to what's important.

For items like smartphones and GPS devices, which will need regular top ups, your best options are a portable power bank or a dynamo and USB charging hub system. Some cyclists take solar-charging devices with them, but these are often impractical and inefficient.

in completing my unbroken journey. Despite the intimidating peaks of the Karakoram, once I was standing beneath them I experienced an equal feeling of satisfaction, gained from having realized a long-held dream.

The instability of a certain region meant that we got a bus out of Pakistan's northern provinces. Once through the urban haze of Islamabad, Lahore and Amritsar, we headed for India's most northerly border, on the Tibetan frontier. Snowy peaks and rocky cols rose up in every direction, and as we moved higher – closer to the belly of the Himalayas – the terrain became ever more arid and inhospitable. But in the four months we spent exploring Central and South Asia, it had become abundantly clear that the special and spectacular were reserved for locations that are, and will hopefully remain, off-road.

The valleys of Himachal Pradesh in India's far north proved to be no different, but the anguish of forcing a fully loaded touring bike over pockmarked tracks of rock and gravel was now so ingrained that I had almost become numb to it. The aching body, blistered fingers, dust-encrusted face and jolting vision were a price we knew we had to pay for the best scenery and most remote quarters.

As we made our way over the gravelly, unmade tracks, we craned our necks for one last look at the mighty peaks before we left them for good. 'See how small you are next to the mountains,' Alain de Botton writes in *The Art of Travel*. 'Accept what is bigger than you and what you do not understand.'

But something can still be fulfilling and worthwhile, even if it is not properly understood. From gazing up at the soaring icy peaks, reflecting on the point of travel between them, and calculating the decision to tackle a rock-hewn, gravel road in a snowstorm at 4,000 m (13,120 ft) above sea level – the mountains had taught us that.

ABOVE Buddhist prayer
flags, tied to posts and draped
across the road, are a common
sight in the Indian, Nepalese
and Bhutanese Himalayas, as
well as in Tibet.

RIGHT Breakfast with
a panoramic view of the
Zarafshan mountain range
in Tajikistan.

LEFT Slowly negotiating our
way to the top of Kunzum La,
a 4,590 m (15,000 ft) pass in
northern India.

ON P. 121 Descending into
the Lahaul valley, India.

ABOVE Waiting for the first rays of sunshine to fend off the autumnal frost in the Spiti valley, India.
LEFT The hubbub of camp, illuminated by the summer sun in the Panj valley, Tajikistan.
OPPOSITE Stopping for repairs in Khorugh, Tajikistan (above), and taking advantage of the local amenities in the Kinnaur valley, India (below).
OVERLEAF Descending from Kunzum La, which separates the Lahaul and Spiti valleys in northern India.

ABOVE Jonny, Rob, Dave and Pete, riding through Tajikistan.
RIGHT Consulting the map to form a plan for the day. The dung on the left is being dried out for later use as fuel.
OPPOSITE Taking in the magnificence of the Karakoram Highway, Gojal valley, Pakistan.

ABOVE Fixing a puncture in the Wakhan valley, Tajikistan, with a young boy keeping us company.
RIGHT The final campsite in the Wakhan valley, before riding up onto the Pamir plateau.
OPPOSITE The early evening sun and a threatening storm make for atmospheric light conditions (above). Warming up in the remote village of Alichur on the Pamir Highway, Tajikistan (below).
OVERLEAF Cycling along the old Hindustan-Tibet Highway in the Kinnaur valley, India.

RIGHT A sandy section of road stops Pete in his tracks. Without the right bike, this kind of surface is simply unrideable.
BELOW Riding beneath the steep cliffs of Tajikistan, with the green slopes of Afghanistan rising up from the other side of the Panj river.
OPPOSITE In the Lahaul valley in northern India, we are forced off our bikes by the steep gradients and unmade roads.

ABOVE Climbing out of the Wakhan valley onto the Pamir plateau on the 4,344 m (14,250 ft) Khargush Pass, Tajikistan.

RIGHT On the Pamir Highway, Rob's bike gives up for good. Despite efforts to fix it, he was forced to hitch a ride all the way to Kyrgyzstan.

OPPOSITE Watching the switchbacks disappear while ascending Kunzum La in Himachal Pradesh, India.

OVERLEAF Blue skies, soaring mountains and smooth tarmac: living the cyclist's dream in the Spiti valley, India.

ABOVE Doing as the locals
do by burning a tersken plant
for warmth. We stopped doing
this once we discovered the
fuel was unsustainable for the
region.

RIGHT Sheltering from
high winds on the road to
Tashkurgan, in the Xinjiang
region of China.

OPPOSITE After leaving
Buddhist northern India,
my bike was decorated with
miniature prayer flags for the
rest of the journey.

OVERLEAF Setting off
on a 60-km (37-mile) ride in
the wrong direction up the
Kokomoron valley, Kyrgyzstan.

ABOVE Approaching the top of the Ak-Baital Pass on the Pamir Highway.
LEFT If you run out of stove fuel, sometimes fire is the only alternative. Naryn region, Kyrgyzstan.
RIGHT After a day of mechanical problems and high-altitude riding, we finally pull off the road and call it a day. Khargush Pass, Tajikistan.

The Tosor Pass, taking us from the expansive Issyk-Kul lake to the high summer
pastures of the eastern Tien Shan mountain range, Kyrgyzstan.

ABOVE A snowstorm moves in as we negotiate the descent of the 4,336 m (14,225 ft) Kyzylart Pass, between the Tajik and Kyrgyz borders.
LEFT Eyeing up the paved tarmac descent of Töö Ashuu. It's downhill all the way to Bishkek, the capital of Kyrgyzstan.
OPPOSITE Progress is slow as we climb out of the Wakhan valley. Behind us are the first peaks of the Hindu Kush, across the border in Afghanistan.
OVERLEAF A post-lunch nap on the Karakoram Highway in Pakistan. Despite being recently rebuilt with huge Chinese investment, the road remains blissfully traffic-free.

ABOVE Making slow progress along the unpaved roads of Himchal Pradesh.
RIGHT One of the countless river crossings that had to be negotiated in the Jilu-Suu valley, Kyrgyzstan.
LEFT 'Ak-Baital Pass. Height 4,655 m [15,270 ft]': the highest pass on the Pamir Highway.
OVERLEAF A long, gradual descent following the river downstream towards the Eki-Naryn gorge in Kyrgyzstan.

ABOVE Words of wisdom graffitied onto a wall near the village of Karimabad, Pakistan.
RIGHT Messages like these are an ever-present feature of the Border Roads Organization in the Indian Himalayas.
OPPOSITE A section of the Hindustan-Tibet Highway, which traces the Kinnaur valley in northern India.
OVERLEAF Climbing ever deeper into the belly of the Himalayas.

ABOVE Two Pakistani lorries roar past, returning from the Khunjerab border with goods from China in a 21st-century version of the Silk Road.

RIGHT Stopping for repairs in Tajikistan. The constant jolting of the road rattled our bikes to pieces.

OPPOSITE A lone car is ferried across the Attabad lake in Pakistan. The lake is the result of a landslide, which submerged an entire village and severed the only road to the north of the country.

OVERLEAF A valid question.

ABOVE Picking a spot –
any spot – in which to camp
in the open expanses of the
Pamir plateau.

OPPOSITE The
inhospitable Pamirs, in
all their cold, harsh and
intimidating beauty.

RIGHT Negotiating the
gravel descent of Kunzum La,
Himachal Pradesh, India.

OVERLEAF On the upper
slopes of Rohtang La, which
separates the green foothills
from the barren Himalaya
proper in northern India.

ON P. 168 Enjoying a
descent in the Wakhan
valley, Tajikistan. Despite
its apparent proximity, the
wall of rock lies on the
other side of the Panj river
in Afghanistan.

TROPICS

SHIMLA, INDIA-GUANGZHOU, CHINA

7,500 KM (4,600 MILES), SEPTEMBER-DECEMBER

INDIA, BANGLADESH, MYANMAR, THAILAND, LAOS, CHINA

TERRAIN: **TARMAC, DIRT, MUD**

FEATURED BIKE: **EXPEDITION**

MOST VALUED ITEM OF KIT: **MOSQUITO REPELLENT**

'CHE-ZU TIN-BAR-TE! THANK YOU!',

I call out to the group of giggling women, who for the last half hour have watched me eat at their roadside café in Myanmar's remote north. The quintessentially Burmese women – with their legs wrapped in *longyi* cloths, faces painted in decorative yellow *thanaka* and teeth stained red with betel leaves, and radiating the easy friendliness that epitomizes Myanmar – wave back. I throw a leg over my bike and ride away from the little hut, which immediately disappears from view, swallowed by the thick undergrowth. I meander past golden temples, decrepit monasteries and remote straw homesteads, but in the sticky heat of the tropics it doesn't take long before I find myself wishing I was back inside the cooling shade of the café, eating my rice and amusing the proprietors with my presence.

I head south on the Kalewa–Monywa road, a road so terrible that the most conventional and often-used route between the two towns is to glide down the Chindwin river. Having suffered with many an ailment in recent days, my companion Pete has been forced to choose the boat, leaving me to navigate the road myself. I begin to track a ridge of relentless inclines and descents, the road a mixture of compacted mud, intermittent asphalt and bizarrely situated cobblestones, and find it particularly testing. Floundering in sweat, dirt and frustration, I throw my bike onto the ground after slipping my foot and kicking the pedal back onto my shin. The mosquitoes, stifling heat, loneliness and pitiful progress have all taken their toll, and I collapse in a frustrated, wincing heap at the side of the road.

A pair of buffalo, festering happily in a pool of mud next to me, return my gaze as I sit there, panting. Their vacant, contented stares are a reminder of the futility of becoming angry in such a situation, and I continue on my way while the buffalo recede into the hot, stuffy nothingness that had preceded my arrival.

• • •

Spread across regions of Africa, the Americas and Asia-Pacific, the tropics form a vital component of the adventure-cycling landscape, providing both a testing environment and highly rewarding travel experience for those who seek them out. Cyclists on longer tours will likely find themselves navigating the tropics on some level, as they occupy much of the central latitudes and often act as a bridge between other climates and terrains. Some tourers also head to the tropical regions exclusively, and – cycling aside – many of the world's most popular tourist destinations are very much tropical. For those who have opted to explore these regions by train or bus in the past, the alternative of a bike is becoming an increasingly popular choice: tourists on a cycle, if you like, rather than cyclists on a tour.

The charm of the tropics lies in the way that, like the rainforests, these regions thrive with colour, diversity and ceaseless activity. While the plants and animals found there are indeed abundant, the humans are equally as absorbing. The band between the Tropics of Cancer and Capricorn is home to some of the most culturally rich and densely populated regions on the planet, and their heat, humidity and rapid growth are reflected in the unrelenting, sometimes suffocating way that humans have colonized these areas. While the remote jungles might be the very embodiment of wildlife on earth, the seething amounts of people across Pakistan, India, China and South East Asia also provided a chaotic cross-section of humanity. The joys and frustrations of travel in the tropics, experienced from the front-row seat of a bicycle, are all the more immersive as a result.

After descending, finally, from the mountains for good, I headed east across northern India, my sunburnt skin fading into a deep brown from endless hours of riding beneath the baking sun. I needed antibiotics for sores that had developed on my cheeks from the combined dirt and heat. My clothes became an increasingly putrid bundle of rags, stiffened by sweat and grime from the road, and my hair – most of which I had chopped off – a bleached, matted mess. There was no escape from either the climate or the abundance of human life, pressing in from every direction. As fatigue began to set in, I discovered a side to the tropics that – when not given a chance to come up for air – could prove suffocating.

With every inch of land already in human use – for habitation, farming or industry – camping, which for so long had provided the chance to unwind and take stock of the day, became impossible. I was forced to look for alternatives, and nights were spent in cheap hotels or in *dhabas* (makeshift roadside establishments, similar to the *chaihanas* of Central Asia, which provided food, shelter and washing facilities for truckers throughout the subcontinent). With the morning start feeling satisfyingly distant, and the light almost gone, I would roll up to my

CHOOSING THE RIGHT BIKE:

EXPEDITION

Expedition bikes are built to withstand it all. Barring the probable exceptions of deep snow or sand, they can be adapted and modified to live up to any conditions. An expedition bike needs to be as suitable for the fast tarmac roads of Europe as for the unpaved mountain tracks of the Himalayas, and be able to carry everything you need for extended periods on the road. They effectively become a portable home, with only the necessary trimmings.

1. FRAME

Steel frames are robust and comfortable, and can be repaired with a simple weld – wherever you are in the world. Lax geometry, with a long wheelbase, and a tall, slack head tube, add comfort and stability. Make sure there is enough tyre clearance for wide, 30–45 mm tyres.

2. WHEEL SIZE

Today it's more likely to be the axle mechanism or inner-tube standard that gives you replacement grief, rather than wheel size. Increased availability and better rolling capabilities lead more and more cyclists to standard 700c wheels.

3. HANDLEBARS

The ability to change weight distribution according to road condition is important, so the choice of handlebars is about ergonomics. Most cyclists tend to go for drop handlebars or butterfly bars, both of which offer a good range of positions.

4. EXTRA BOSSES

Most expedition bikes come with extra bosses for bottle cages, mudguards, pumps or spare spokes.

5. DYNAMO HUB

A dynamo generator in the front hub is a common feature, often powering a front light and charging electrics via a USB.

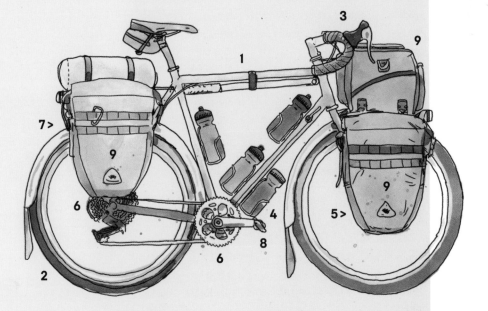

6. LARGE GEAR VARIATION

Tarmacked descents and gravel passes require very different gear choices. For these, try a 46/36/24 chainset combination and a 12/36 or 11/32 cassette.

7. BRAKES

Disc brakes perform better and are less likely to go wrong; rim brakes are easier to bodge if broken. Unless you're sure you'll be able to repair a disc, go for cantilever rim brakes.

8. PEDALS

Chances are you're going to be spending as much time off the bike as on it, so choose shoes and cleats carefully, or substitute with flats and hiking shoes instead.

9. LUGGAGE

For a fully loaded expedition bike, four panniers and a rack pack are the tried and true setup, although some cyclists prefer trailers or cargo bikes. (See pp. 260–1 for a full kit list.)

STAYING
HEALTHY

Prolonged periods away from running water and aids to cleanliness will always come at a cost to personal health, so do your best to ensure access to them. Below are some tips to help you enjoy your ride to the full.

Use alcohol gel for washing hands
Wet wipes can be useful for other parts
Be wary of meat, fish, dairy and uncooked veg
Swallow your concerns if you think raising them will cause offence

Wash clothes, particularly cycling shorts, regularly
Purify water with a pump or effervescent tablets
Collect water from a natural spring or stream as high up as possible, especially if animals are grazing nearby
Avoid drinking from larger rivers
Always take advantage of chances to refuel and rehydrate

Depending on the type of tour you are undertaking, some items to include in your first-aid kit are:
Bandages and plasters
Medical tape
Alcohol wipes
Scissors
Painkillers
Tablets for diarrhoea
Gel plasters for blisters
Iodine
Antihistamines

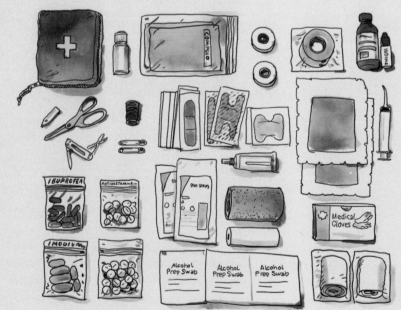

chosen *dhaba* – grotty enough to accommodate myself and my *saikil* without fuss, but with enough lorries parked outside to know it wasn't a totally woebegone arrangement. It later transpired that Pete, who was riding two days behind me after being delayed in Delhi with visa problems, had chosen the same *dhabas* on a couple of occasions. At one of them I had been made to pose for a photo with the owners, which had then been shown to Pete when he turned up a day or two later – no doubt to the surprise and amusement of all.

The joy of the *dhaba* clientele was that it couldn't care less if I was there or not, which in densely populated India – where crowds of 20 or more would gather to watch whenever you dismounted your bike – offered welcome anonymity. English was generally out of the question, but the silent connection shared while washing at the communal water troughs out front was something to savour. Lit up by headlights in the falling dusk, with the road roaring behind us, we washed away the dirt and intensity of the day in the cooling water. It seemed that regardless of race or mode of transport or my unexpected presence as a foreigner, washing was a basic, ritualistic task that we could all appreciate as much as the next person.

The Grand Trunk Road is the main artery of northern India, an ancient trade route spanning the subcontinent. Picking it up in New Delhi, I followed it for a near 2,000-km (1,240-mile) stretch through Varanasi, Kolkata and Dhaka in Bangladesh. Eventually we emerged in the often forgotten, less travelled northeast of India, known as the 'Seven Sister States'. The increasingly hilly terrain and steadily encroaching rainforest, which began to envelop us as we pushed on into this remote and forgotten corner of Asia, meant that the population began to drop off rapidly, bringing with it an immediate feeling of tranquillity.

The effects of the monsoon season were still making themselves felt as we traced the road eastward. Churned up and imprinted with tyre treads by the rain, the once clay-like mess had solidified into a corrugated washboard

KEEPING DRY
IN THE WET

If you will be cycling over a prolonged period of time, especially in tropical regions, then chances are you're going to get rained on. Sometimes it is best to just run for cover if showers are short and regular. If getting wet is unavoidable, however, there are precautions you can take to avoid it becoming overly problematic.

Use plenty of dry bags, from big ones for tents, sleeping bags and clothes, to smaller ones for valuables and money. Otherwise use regular plastic bags or bin liners. **Fit mudguards:** there's no way of stopping rain from falling from the sky, but mudguards ensure that excess water will not spray up from below.

Dress appropriately: if it's cold and wet, wear woollen clothing, which retains its insulative properties when wet. If it's warm and wet, synthetic materials will dry more quickly. **Overshoes,** a type of waterproof sock that fits over ordinary shoes or cycling boots, can make a real difference in helping to avoid getting wet feet in the rain.

Avoid packing a wet tent: give it a shake, hang it up for a while, pack it last. **Avoid faffing: the more times you open your bags, the more chance there is for moisture to get in.** Pitch your tent on higher ground, away from water. **Dry wet gear by taking advantage of any breaks in the weather and strapping it to your panniers.**

– the bane of cycle tourists worldwide. Passing traffic rattled up plumes of fine sediment, turning the carriageway into a choking dust bowl. The aftermath of the monsoon season and its effect on the roads were factors we had not planned for, but luckily we were able to continue uncompromised. A few weeks earlier, much of the road network would have been a sloppy, impassable quagmire, and all but impossible to navigate by bike. Arriving now meant that our means of transport was back to being merely unusual.

Dense jungle, combined with the endlessly hilly terrain, had evidently made building roads in these regions difficult, and the small, unnavigable rivers, although abundant, were of no use as infrastructure. As a result, some highly remote regions began to pass under our wheels. While the deserts, high-altitude plateaux and rugged mountains of the world had provided outwardly empty visions of remoteness, we discovered that the tropics offered a somewhat different view: closeness replaced space, claustrophobia replaced disconnectedness, trees replaced bare ground. Somehow this made whatever lay beyond feel even further away, guarded by layer upon layer of rainforest.

Roads had no option but to trace the rivers, piggybacking onto the natural course they carved through the otherwise impenetrable forest. The undergrowth butted up against one side of the road like a wall, while the other crumbled away into the gently flowing brown water, before the jungle rose up again on the opposite bank. Road and river, the only two avenues of movement in an environment of restrictive space, snaked in unison in opposite directions through the abyss. In one direction rode a cycle tourist, heading ever deeper into the jungle in search of the pass to the next valley; in the other, driftwood was carried downstream.

'Going up that river was like travelling back to the earliest beginnings of the world, when vegetation rioted on the earth and the big trees were kings,' wrote Joseph Conrad in *The Heart of Darkness*, a novel forever bound to the jungle experience. I thought of it as I peered into the trees beside me, which ate away at the manmade road, yet found themselves eroded and swept away by the river. 'An empty stream, a great silence, an impenetrable forest. The air was warm, thick, heavy, sluggish. There was no joy in the brilliance of sunshine.'

Every now and then, sporadic stretches of tarmac would provide some respite or a cluster of wooden buildings would appear at the side of the road, offering the opportunity to collect clean water and buy food. In these former colonial parts, there was even a fair chance of meeting an English speaker. Inhabitants of the region, bordered on three sides by Myanmar, China and Bhutan, seemed far removed from their compatriots in the plains west of Bangladesh, but the coagulation of mountains, rainforests and disputed borders had disrupted the flow of ethnicity and culture enough for us to wonder to what extent they were compatriots at all.

Apart from these intermittent settlements, we were days from any major urban hub, and the top of each climb was rewarded with an endless panorama of rainforest, leaving us with the elation of being in a part of the world most people have probably never heard of. Many know the old riddle: if a tree falls in a forest and there's nobody around to hear, does it make a sound? What about a cyclist who rides through a place that doesn't 'exist' – on Google, in travel brochures or in magazines? Adventure cycle touring is about discovering these places, making them real and vivid in your mind and experience, and taking your memories of them away with you.

After almost two months, and having ridden through the highs and lows of what had been an utterly immersive country, we left India for good. To get into Myanmar through the Moreh–Tamu border point we had to get a special permit, a typical example of the forethought and planning required in long-distance touring. While there is a time and a place for the romantic ideal of following your nose, in this case we had to begin the application process back in Delhi, stating the exact time and date

TIMING THE SEASONS

Taking the seasons into account is an important part of planning any bike tour. Avoiding summer in the desert, winter in the mountains or monsoon season in the tropics could mean the difference between euphoria and misery when you're living outside for 24 hours a day, and variations in altitude and the speed at which you plan to travel will complicate the issue further. In order to avoid a Himalayan winter, I realized I would have to endure a European one, and even then I was late – after being delayed by visas, some passes had nearly closed by the time I arrived. Some cyclists choose to follow the seasons, altering their route to follow the warmer, drier climes around the globe. If you don't have that flexibility, then planning, and compromise, is essential.

we intended to cross the border – and paying a substantial fee while we were at it – thousands of kilometres and many weeks beforehand. But the permit was never emailed over, and so, armed only with our visas and a telephone number, we arrived at the border and were told to sit and wait. After being telephoned, a man eventually appeared on a motorbike, and after some transaction between him and the officials, we were rushed through – no papers required.

'Enjoy Myanmar,' said our mysterious fixer, before hopping back on his bike and careering off down the dusty track, leaving us slightly suspicious about the legitimacy of our fees and whether the permits had been needed at all – or were just a myth perpetuated by travellers like us, desperate to do all they could to keep the doors of onward progress open.

As with countless other border crossings, transport links and run-ins with both state and vigilante officials, we had learned when and when not to resist. Paying a questionable permit fee somehow felt different to paying off the Kyrgyz policemen who accused us of drug trafficking and threatened to withhold our passports until we handed over some dollars (we didn't, after a 45-minute interrogation). It is necessary to accept that occasionally there will be certain games to play, and sometimes you'll be taken for a ride, but on this occasion we had gained entry into a country that for years had been closed and under the control of a military junta. We were lucky to be able to cross overland, regardless of how we got in.

Abandoning the fake itinerary we had concocted for the permit, and cancelling the hotels we had needed to book for our visas, we set off into the untouched lands of northern Myanmar and quickly encountered unmade, muddy roads, suffocating heat and swathes of jungle. Leaving the border crossing felt like setting sail from a deserted island. A castaway knows that he will be able to sustain himself for a period, potentially indefinitely, but he also knows that time in the outside world is ticking away. This is the thorn in the side of the long-distance

WILD CAMPING SURVIVAL GUIDE

Camping in the wild can be an intimidating prospect for the uninitiated, but in time the experience becomes second nature, letting you enjoy it for the great experience it is.

Try to respect the rules of wild camping in any given place – wherever possible, that is: if you need to sleep, you need to sleep. **Asking for permission can be a good way to start, as you'll soon know whether or not** it's a problem. People might think you're a little strange, but generally will be happy to let you bed down. This is especially true if the weather is bad and sheltering in a farm building or garage would be useful.

If you decide not to ask permission, inconspicuousness is key. Wait until dusk, when people are on their way home or already inside, before looking for a campsite. Try to coincide this with leaving a settlement, where you picked up supplies for the night.

Once you've identified a potential location, make sure no one's around and exit the road quickly, then hang around for 10 minutes or so. If anyone has seen you, they'll quickly make it known if they have a problem. Check the area for potential hazards: flash floods, ants and other animals, etc.

If you're disturbed, have a plan of action that goes beyond pretending to be asleep. Knowing words like 'friend', 'no problem' and 'safe' in the local language can be useful.

Be respectful of your campsite location and take your rubbish with you. **Get up and out early.**

COOKING
SETUPS

Most adventure cyclists will carry some sort of portable kitchen with them. Anything beyond a stove, a pan or two, a knife, a spoon and some water can probably be considered unnecessary, but if you have the space, things like oil, seasoning and a scouring pad can be useful. As far as stoves go, there are three popular options:

MULTIFUEL STOVES

MSR WhisperLite and Primus Omnifuel models are favoured by long-distance tourers for their robustness. They will run on anything flammable (petrol, diesel, methylated spirits, kerosene, white gas), and are a good option as petrol (often known as benzene) is widely available. Bear in mind, however, that low octane ratings are bad for the stove. Pans and stove will routinely get covered in dirty soot, so regular maintenance is essential.

SPIRIT STOVES

Trangia stoves have a simple, robust design and use very clean fuel (alcohol or methylated spirits). You can make your own from an empty beer can.

GAS STOVES

MSR Pocket Rocket, Jetboil and Campingaz are favoured by tourers on shorter tours in non-remote regions. Gas stoves also use clean fuel (propane, butane), and have an adjustable flame for quick boiling. Canisters are only readily available in certain areas, such as Europe and the US.

self-supported cycle tourist, who enjoys all the freedom in the world on one hand, but is a slave to his own ambition and independence on the other, and must accept that covering every inch of the journey by pedal power often comes at the price of a restrictive schedule. The comforts of a desert island must always be deserted.

We slowly poached in the layer of sweat that soaked our clothes as daytime temperatures sat between 35 and 40° C (95 and 104° F), with humidity at some godforsaken height. The slightest shadow provided by the undergrowth was pounced upon, as we tried in vain to escape the relentless torment of the sun. Darkness fell at around six o'clock, but well before then – even before we had time to finish our instant noodles – we were forced to seek refuge in our stifling tents on account of the swarms of mosquitoes that descended at dusk.

'You still awake?' I would call out, after hours spent trying to sleep, while simultaneously fanning myself, all the while dreading the buzzing that signalled the arrival of a bloodsucking airborne intruder.

'Of course,' came the immediate reply.

'How much do you wish you were shivering in a mountain blizzard right now?'

'We'll be in Thailand soon. There'll be air-con, fresh food, cold beer, tarmac roads. It's going to be … Oh shit, there's one in here.'

Thailand, and later Laos and China, did indeed provide a far easier passage through regions that were still very much tropical. While it is still possible to get off the beaten track in South East Asia, the main roads are often surfaced with smooth, comfortable stretches of asphalt, making long distances more attainable and the struggle to navigate them less tiring. A good road network is also indicative of advancements in other areas, and we found ourselves enjoying the relative luxuries these more developed areas offered. We no longer had to spend hours pushing and pulling our bikes through stretches of mud, sand or rock, and took great pleasure in the abundance of restaurants, eateries and food stalls that lined the roads. I hadn't experienced such easygoing, comfortable travel conditions for months, and, as well as being very welcome, it was something to remember if we ever fancied a version of cycle touring that gave the option of a bit of luxury mixed in with the hardship.

Four months after exiting Xinjiang province into Pakistan, I crossed back into China via the southwestern Yunnan province. Dense rainforest, banana plantations and tight spurs of interlocking valleys replaced the empty, arid high-altitude deserts and mountain ranges I remembered. Where before the air had been dry and the skies clear, the weather was now wet, grey and increasingly cold. Tropical storms are fierce but thankfully brief, and as I moved further north I found myself continually plagued by them, forced to take shelter in buildings or under trees until they passed. The raindrops were so big and heavy that you could pick out individual ones, as they plummeted to the ground before imploding.

Cycling in such conditions was unpleasant at best, and downright dangerous at worst, so I was only too happy to spend a few minutes with the locals, taking refuge in whatever nook was available and – because you can take the Brit out of Britain, but you can't take Britain out of the Brit – sharing jokes about the weather.

After a good length of time of being able to communicate with locals, whether in Russian in Central Asia or in English throughout the subcontinent and South East Asia, China proved a wall of silence. Not a word of English was spoken anywhere, and despite some effort in learning the basics, my Mandarin remained mostly unintelligible. Even through body language communication seemed difficult, and I found that many people would not even try to understand even the most basic of charades (pointing at mouth for 'hungry' or 'need water'; raising hands to one side of face for 'tired', etc).

With Pete ending his trip in Bangkok, another friend, Jonny, had flown out to meet me, and together we were able to laugh off the isolation created by the language barrier. Using each other as a crutch – one tired and travel weary, but rejuvenated by the presence of a companion; the other overwhelmed by the transition between London and rural China, but grateful for the experience of the other – we headed east.

Our journey took us from poor, agrarian villages, where farmers ploughed their fields with horses, to towns that appeared on the map as a mere junction, but which in fact were cities of hundreds of thousands of people. In time, the mountainous tropical forests metamorphosed into hills lined with regimented crops of tea plantations, then into glistening rice paddies, and finally into a mix of low, forested hills and intermittent cities. The tribal dresses and ethnically distinctive faces of the tropics, too, became lost to the march of urbanized grey modernity of eastern China.

The towering trees, stuffy heat and overcrowded spaces of the tropical rainforest were gradually replaced by the towering buildings, polluted air and overcrowded urban centres, pulsating with life. A steady stream of ever-bigger cities began to appear, and with conurbations containing tens of millions of people still to negotiate before the Hong Kong border, the intense, suffocating jungle was set to turn distinctly urban.

ABOVE Finishing a cup
of tea to the amusement of the
locals in Bodhgaya, India.
RIGHT In the suffocating
heat of the tropics, tasks
like truing a wheel become all
the more irritating.
LEFT A typically Indian scene,
complete with decaying façade,
tropical backdrop and *saikil*
(pronounced 'cycle').
OVERLEAF Riding the
backroads of southern
Myanmar at dusk. What better
way to spend an evening?
ON P. 185 Karstic limestone
rock formations, covered
with the subtropical forests of
Guangxi province, China.

ABOVE Rice paddies in Uttar Pradesh, India, as the intense heat of another day in the tropics finally begins to recede.
LEFT An inescapable side effect of riding in the heat and humidity: sweat, and lots of it.
OPPOSITE Negotiating the dry, dusty roads of the remote backwaters of Assam (above). Dense jungle cloaks the hillside in Manipur, India (below).
OVERLEAF Having been advised to leave Bangladesh, and suffering a terminal wheel failure on the way to the customs post, we were offered a lift in the back of a pickup truck to ensure we arrived before the border closed.

ABOVE The temple-strewn landscape of Bagan, Myanmar.
RIGHT An offering of *betel quid* (areca nut, lime and tobacco, wrapped in a betel leaf), ubiquitous throughout the Indian subcontinent.
OPPOSITE Making our way through the sticky evening heat at the end of another day in the Assamese jungle, India.
OVERLEAF Rice paddies are a staple view when riding through tropical regions.

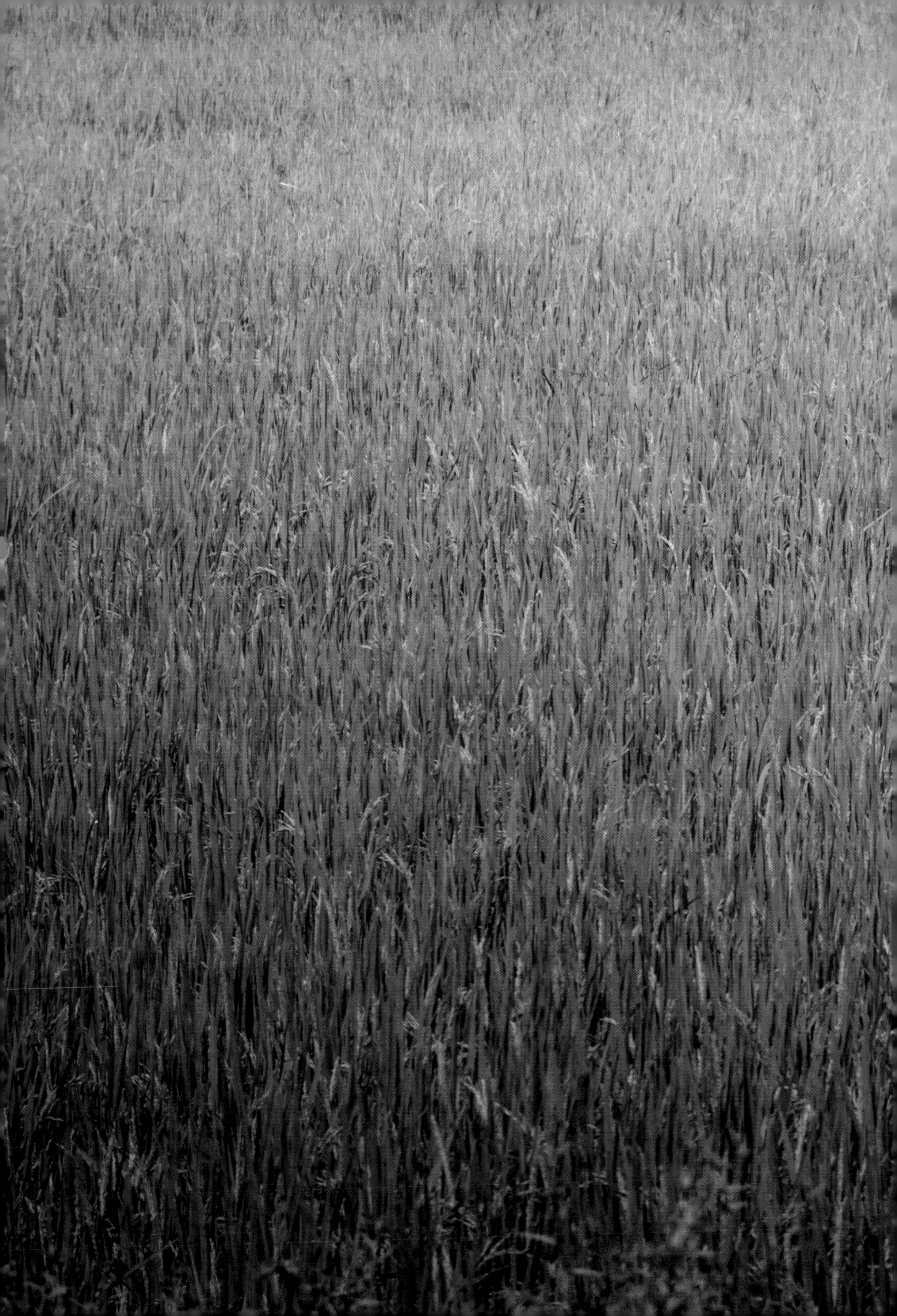

ABOVE Wild camping in a sugarcane plantation, with the distinctive karstic rock formations of Guilin, China, in the background.

RIGHT The warm glow of evening fades to a hue that tells me it's time to stop and find a campsite.

OPPOSITE Picking my way along the endless road between Kalewa and Monywa in Myanmar, with nothing but trees for company.

OVERLEAF Old meets new in China: a flock of goats being shepherded along a modern tarmac road.

ABOVE A Laotian village, nestled in a steaming valley near the Chinese border.
RIGHT Water, water, everywhere: loading the bikes onto a ferry at Yangshuo, China.
OPPOSITE Tiny villages and steeply pitched roads, crisscrossing the karstic landscape near Guilin.
OVERLEAF A quick scout about in the undergrowth in Yunnan province reveals the perfect campsite, just above the road.

ABOVE Following an undefined track in Guangxi region, China, in search of a campsite.

LEFT Rhesus macaque monkeys in Shimla, India, always ready to pounce on unsuspecting cyclists from the shadows.

RIGHT The dramatic limestone landscape surrounding Luang Prabang, in northern Laos.

OVERLEAF Setting up the tents and starting dinner before the mosquitoes descend in southern Myanmar.

ABOVE Pete rides up alongside a work elephant – to the surprise of its rider – in northeast India.
RIGHT We have some company on the road.
OVERLEAF The subtropical forests, maze-like valleys and endless winding roads of Himachal Pradesh, India.

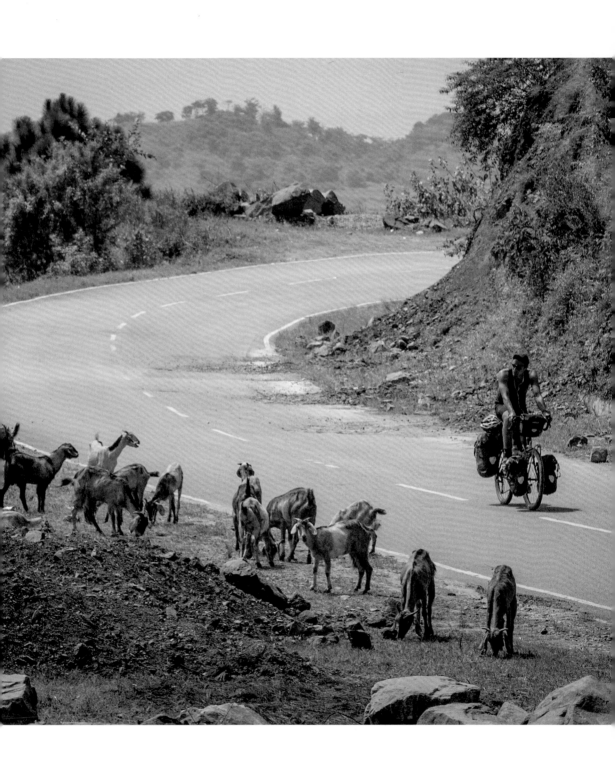

ABOVE Hot, tired and sweaty on the Grand Trunk Road in Pakistan.

RIGHT An unexpected spot of sunshine at the end of a stormy day in Yunnan, China.

LEFT Another long, gradual climb, this time enjoying the cooler air of southern China in December.

ON P. 216 Making an early start in Punjab, India, to get some kilometres in before the real heat of the day.

5

CITIES

GUANGZHOU, CHINA–HONG KONG, CHINA

200 KM (124 MILES), DECEMBER

TERRAIN: TARMAC, CONCRETE

FEATURED BIKE: ULTRALIGHT ADVENTURE BIKE

MOST VALUED ITEM OF KIT: GPS NAVIGATION DEVICE

'60KM' READS THE SIGN ABOVE MY HEAD.

I stop by the side of the road to give myself time to decipher the characters, and eventually work out that they denote the sound 'Shen Jen': 60 km (37 miles) to Shenzhen, I think to myself – fantastic. My speedometer tells me I've come 70 km (43 miles) since leaving my hostel in Guangzhou, but while the distance suggests that they are different cities, in reality Shenzhen and Guangzhou are just two opposite ends of a sprawling megalopolis. I am somewhere between them, in the middle of a third, Dongguan.

Legions of identical highrises – apartment blocks, offices, empty concrete lattices – rise up in every direction, disappearing into the smog. The eight-lane carriageway I'm riding along is filled with trucks, scooters, clapped-out old wagons and expensive imported cars.

I weave between pedestrians and produce stalls at the side of the road, inhaling the clouds of soot that belch out from the HGVs. My reflection, glimpsed dancing across the windows of buildings in the centre of Shenzhen, appears incongruous with the scene around me. Glamorously dressed, briefcase-wielding people strut along the pavement, while I resemble some sort of cycling hobo, wearing torn, dirty clothes, shoes with holes that reveal my toes, and a tan that is as likely to be the product of ground-in dirt as of the sun's rays.

The bike that rolls beneath me is on its last legs, and doesn't owe me a kilometre. I have been thinking this for thousands of kilometres; small fixes or simple ignorance have been just about able to keep it carrying me forward. By now it is unable to change gear and the braking system barely engages, but I have already employed my spare cables to attach my panniers, whose fitment mechanisms have all snapped off. Patches of rust appear on the frame where sweat has corroded through the paintwork, and the lack of a rear mudguard – broken and discarded long ago – has left everything encased in a thick layer of grime. The only traces of colour are the Tibetan prayer flags that flutter from my handlebars, and I cannot help but feel that their peaceful messages are at odds with the skyscrapers around me.

• • •

Cities and urban areas are often an inescapable part of any cycling adventure. With their pollution, busy streets, comparative unfriendliness and lack of natural beauty, ithey represent the antithesis of what you would assume cycle tourists go in search of when they set off on an adventure. But while there is a lot of truth in that, it would be foolish to remain blind to the benefits cities offer. Their role as the most diverse melting pots of human life on the planet, where cultures, religions, languages and food meet, is easy to forget when you live in one yourself and have become accustomed to its diversity.

When transplanted from your own city to the hustle and bustle of one in a foreign country, this admirable characteristic becomes a lot more apparent, especially when viewed from the vantage point of a bicycle. Few places was this more visibly tangible than in Kashgar, an outpost in China's far west. Like Istanbul, and Samarkand before it, Kashgar had been a much-anticipated Silk Road visit. With food, clothing, architecture and faces woven together from the tapestry of Eurasian history, more so than anywhere else along the Silk Road, Kashgar was where I felt its narrative most palpably.

After cycling through the neighbouring regions, observing their different characteristics, I found I was able to ride past as many distinguishable locales in one street as had previously taken months. The unibrows of Tajikistan, the dresses of Uzbekistan, the hats of Kyrgyzstan, the languages of Turkey, Persia and the Far East could all be found within 50 m (164 ft) of any of the city's bazaars, along with sightings of blonde and ginger hair, freckles and blue eyes, mixed in with the epicanthic folds of Asia and the dark complexions of the Middle East. As I rode through the city's fabled streets, I wondered at the empires, pilgrimages and trade routes that had led to such an assorted mix of people.

There is no doubt that pedalling through sparsely populated, remote parts of the world, followed by diverse human-infested channels of it, reveals layers of socio-logical and cultural identity that might otherwise go unnoticed. But incorporating cities into an adventure also has a very real and practical upside: while we may escape by bike in search of dramatic panoramas, wild jungles and empty deserts, it does not take long for both body and mind to begin lusting after the comforts that are to be found in urban areas.

I was first struck by this thought during the run-in to Istanbul, while suffering the cold and fatigue of a European winter. Even before I arrived in the city, I felt as though I understood it. After six weeks of cycling, through most meteorological conditions and with a mindset of

CHOOSING THE RIGHT BIKE:

ULTRALIGHT

A lightweight touring setup should be as minimal as possible: the less you pack, the quicker you'll be able to leave and the further you'll be able to travel. Deciding what is and isn't essential will depend on the tour: too much stuff will elevate the setup to something more than 'ultralight'. Bikepacking bags offer the best luggage option, as their compact size forces you to pack sparingly and keeps the bike manoeuvrable. Preferred by ultra-distance racers, weekend overnighters and lightweight tourers alike.

1. FRAME

Depending on the circumstances (ride location, type), ultralight setups make the most of the benefits of steel, aluminium or carbon.

More important is the geometry, which should be relaxed for maximum comfort and versatility. Gravel, cyclocross or comfortable road bikes are ideal.

2. FRAME BAG

For storing heavier items, such as tool kits, spares, electrics and food. Extra clothes and a tent can also be stored inside the frame bag.

3. TOP-TUBE BAG

This is where your valuable and/or essential items (phone, wallet, passport, snacks, and so on) go for easy access.

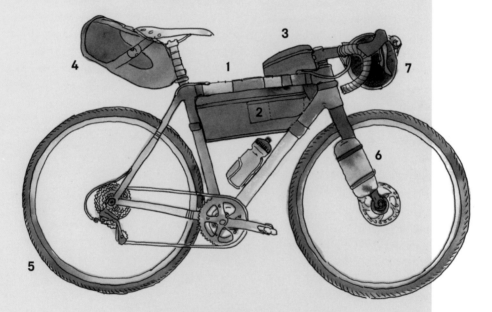

4. SADDLEBAG

You don't want too much weight this high up on the bike or swinging around beneath you, so keep the saddlebag free for lightweight clothes.

5. VERSATILE TYRES

Being able to cover long distances, as well as get off the beaten path, requires an adaptable tyre; 28–35 mm (1–1¼ in.) and with a little grip is ideal.

6. FORK LUGGAGE

If you can't fit all of your stuff into your bags, fork-boss attachments can provide some extra storage space.

7. BAR BAG

Conveniently rolled up into a neat cylinder and strapped to your handlebars, this is the perfect place for sleeping and bivvy bags.

TRANSPORTATION

Apart from overnighters and weekenders, few trips will begin and end at your front door, so navigating public transport with a bicycle in tow will more than likely be a factor, both at home and abroad.

PLANES

Book it on, usually as large sports equipment (although sometimes the option for bicycle is given). Dismantle the bike by removing the handlebar/stem and twist under the top tube, removing pedals and saddle, taking out the wheels and removing and securing the rear derailleur. Source a bike box (try local bike shops), and pack your bike with plenty of padding; the rest of your kit – panniers, clothes, etc. – can be put to good use here. If riding directly to the airport with the intention of putting your bike on a plane, research ahead of time if the airline will allow this, and if so, what packaging resources they provide. If forced to, could you make your own bike box from scraps of cardboard? (Answer: Yes). If flying in and out of the same city, try and find somewhere to leave your bike box for the return leg.

TRAINS AND BUSES

More commonly used than planes, with some borders necessitating bus transfers and trains being useful for making up ground quickly. Generally less strict than airlines, but can be a hassle, so research specific locations ahead of time. The bike will generally either be on its side in the hold or lashed to the roof. Make sure the drive side is facing upwards to avoid damage.

TAXIS

Occasionally you'll need to be resourceful, and in emergencies it might be necessary to employ the services of random people and their vehicles for transport. In some (usually remoter) places, 'taxi' can be a loose term to describe the lift-sharing services of car-owning locals. Here is a step-by-step guide: 1) hail vehicle; 2) explain situation; 3) settle price; 4) strap bike to roof; 5) hop in. It is handy to have some lengths of rope on hand for such situations.

luxury-depriving frugality, I was utterly exhausted and in need of rest. So more than reading about how and why Istanbul (or Constantinople before that, and Byzantium before that) had come to command such significance in history, in my desperate need to stop and recuperate, I could actually feel it. As a traveller between east and west, like the many millions before me, I was always destined to stop there, contribute my time and money to it, and add my name to the list of those who have come before and made the city what it is.

Of course, a city need not be home to millions of people for it to have the same effect. While small, the oasis settlements of Khiva and Bukhara had evoked a similar sense of connection in the Uzbekistan deserts, as had arrival in the tiny remote town of Murghab, high up on the Pamir plateau in Tajikistan. These, and countless settlements beyond them, had all explained their place on the map simply by virtue of how comparatively difficult existence was outside of them, away from the patch of sheltered land, river confluence or naturally high ground that had initially nurtured colonization. It is only when arriving by bike (or perhaps on foot) that you are truly able to appreciate this.

After rolling up to a city in a bedraggled mess, having spent days or weeks on the road, the comforts of such a place are immeasurable. Readily available food and drink, the prospect of sleeping in a bed, people to interact with and the buzz of activity are relished in the same way that their antitheses had been previously. As well as recuperation for the body and mind, in a practical sense cities also provide the chance to reconnect with people, contact friends and family at home, research onward routes, deal with permits or visas, back up photos and recharge electricals – all things that remain blissfully out of mind when crossing the spaces in between.

The reverse of this is also true, of course, and throughout my trip I found that during extended periods in cities their comforts would begin to wear thin. In Luxembourg City, Sarajevo, Thessaloniki and Istanbul, it hadn't taken long before the sheer excitement of the road ahead lured me back onto it. Spending too much time in Bishkek, Kyrgyzstan, made me realize that after six months of bike travel my perception of normality had altered to the point where if I wasn't racking up kilometres and exploring the world via a string of wild camping spots, then I was unsatisfied, and I flew through the city as if my bike had grown a motor. Later on, during an 1,800-km (1,118-mile) stint between New Delhi and Dhaka on the unending urban mayhem that is the Grand Trunk Road, my daily routine – despite involving bike travel – became a suffocating struggle of noise, dirt and fatigue.

'All the world going and coming,' wrote Rudyard Kipling, a longtime resident of India, of this road in *Kim*. 'It is to me as a river from which I am withdrawn like a log after a flood. Truly the Grand Trunk Road is a wonderful spectacle. It runs straight, bearing without crowding India's traffic for fifteen hundred miles – such a river of life as nowhere else exists in the world.'

It has no doubt changed somewhat since then – it is certainly not without crowding these days – but the sentiment remains as true as ever. In its own way, it is indeed spectacular – an archetype of raw, ungoverned urban chaos. With Kabul, Peshawar, Lahore, Amritsar, Delhi, Agra, Varanasi, Kolkata and Dhaka all forming waypoints along its path, it is indeed a 'river of life' that cannot be found anywhere else in the world. Too long spent cycling on it, however, will wear you thin against its unrelenting intensity.

The level of involvement that bike travel forces you to have with your surroundings is a wonderful thing, but there are some environments in which the drawbacks are clear, and riding for almost 2,000 km (1,242 miles) through the industrial north of India proved one of them. But even though there are certain characteristics, shared by urban areas universally, which do not resonate well with cycle tourists, it is only when you arrive by bike, having first experienced everything before it, that you are able to recognize this fact. Throughout my journey, I came to realize that the cities and the regions that separate them share something of a symbiotic relationship: one cannot be fully appreciated without the other.

My route south, through the motorway mazes and glass-fronted business districts of China's megacities, echoed the notion that cities and adventure cycling do not match. But they can be negotiated, mentally and physically, and are a worthy contribution on the itinerary of any cycle tour. I was happy that Hong Kong would draw the curtain on this one. Like the other cities I had passed through before it, Hong Kong had the visible evidence of a place that draws in the cultures and people of the regions around it. It was a truly cosmopolitan city, and for that diversity, and coming together of places that had once been so distant, I cannot help but liken it to the adventure-cycling landscape of today.

If Thomas Stevens set the foundation of adventure cycling in the 19th century (see p. 10), then Hong Kong illustrates how far it has evolved since. There are now myriad avenues of potential, in the form of tour locations, bike setups, luggage categories and attainable distances, and ideas of what it is to have an adventure on two wheels, with new directions being built and realized all the time.

Within this community are the hardcore extremists, who think nothing of dragging their bikes across the Tibetan plateau or Gobi desert and will only countenance tours that are at least four years in length. Then there are the traditionalists, with their drop-handlebar touring bikes and wax-cotton panniers, who might spend months beforehand poring over maps and gathering equipment, and amble along country lanes before pitching their tents in some fair meadow – that is, if they can't find an official camping ground.

The edgy bikepacking set thrives on nimbleness of bike and of mind – not having the means to overpack for the long haul, but not wanting to either. This group is after intense bursts of adventure, and straps its packs to whatever bike is available, before heading for the hills with efficiency. And then there are those who like to embark on point-to-point-to-point cycling adventures with hardly any belongings at all, taking only a change of clothes, a toothbrush, a phone charger and a bivvy bag at most.

The adventure racers have recently begun showing up, too, bringing carbon-fibre, tight-fitting Lycra and exhausting speeds with them. They've got the lumberjack shirt-wearing tourers re-addressing their wardrobes in the interests of practicality, and their style of racing has begun to tempt the diehard road cyclists into parts of the city that contain panniers, maps and knobby tyres. This is a breed that sees itself in the Audax and Randonneur demographic, but have put a 21st-century twist on these niche forms of organized long-distance riding, and their calendar of adventure races continues to grow by the year. But the city is fluid, and these tribes of adventure cyclists do not feel restricted to the areas they first inhabited. Blending together ideas, bikes, luggage and destinations, while keeping the same mindset of a two-wheeled explorer, the community is evolving and maturing their environment to ever-greater heights.

Climbing Tai Mo Shan, the highest peak in Hong Kong, was the final obstacle before the finish, and approaching its upper slopes from the north, I passed a group of 'Brompton tourers', who had taken their folding bikes, initially designed for the train-bound commuter, and attached lightweight bikepacking luggage systems to them. No doubt escaping the sea of highrises to explore the New Territories, or China beyond, their appearance reminded me of a former life, and whole days spent out in the saddle on smaller adventures.

I felt refreshed by their presence, for while my adventure had been years in the making, theirs were probably no longer than a few days, and yet the two experiences were fuelled by the same desire to get out and see something, achieve something, feel something. I had been lucky enough to find myself in circumstances where cycling from the UK to Hong Kong was a realistic undertaking, and dedicating myself to an entire year in the saddle had

POPULAR
ROUTES
WORLDWIDE

EUROPE

With the amount of paved roads in Europe, you really can go anywhere and undertake a near-infinite number of trip variants. There are some 'classics', however, with the Alps being an obvious favourite. Others are the EuroVelo routes (see p. 258), and Nordkapp to Gibraltar, which crosses Europe from its most northerly point to its most southerly.

ASIA

From Turkey there are two routes east to Central Asia: through Iran, or through the Caucasus and across the Caspian Sea. From here, most people head either in the direction of Mongolia and China, or (less frequently) south over the Karakoram Highway to Pakistan. The north of India and Nepal are more popular than the southern regions of the subcontinent, while Myanmar's recent 'opening' means that it is now possible to link India with South East Asia. With its fairly porous borders, cheap living costs and balmy climate, the mainland countries form a touring hotspot, while Indonesia, Japan and Korea are popular island destinations.

AFRICA

Africa's two main unbroken long-distance routes are centred around the eastern and western parts of the continent. Starting in Morocco, you can head south through West Africa and the Kalahari, or start in Egypt and follow the Nile down to Ethiopia, then through Kenya and Tanzania towards the Cape of Good Hope.

AMERICAS

While the Pan-American Highway, stretching between Ushuaia in Argentina and Prudhoe Bay, Alaska, is the 'big one', the Patagonia region and Andes mountain range serve as South America's most popular destination. As for the US, the Great Divide serves as a famous north–south trail; the Trans-America Trail runs east to west.

AUSTRALIA AND NEW ZEALAND

The remoteness of inland Australia means that it is quite restrictive for potential routes, so segments of the 15,000 km (9,321 mile)-long perimeter, as well as diversions to Alice Springs, form the basis of many tours. In New Zealand, a simple north–south traverse is well known as one of the best rides in the world.

been a pleasure and a privilege. Finishing, however, would mean starting a new chapter, in which such adventures would likely be undertaken in smaller chunks.

I was relieved about that, too, as a year on the road had left me feeling as though I needed an escape in the other direction. While riding had filled the slot – mentally and physically – of 'work', I missed the satisfaction and sense of identity that comes with paid employment. I missed casual conversation, free of language barriers, polite small talk and questions about my bike. I missed not having the opportunity to get to know anybody (such is the transience of constant travel), and I missed those I had known before leaving, whom I had said goodbye to so many months ago.

Upon descending from the mountain, my aerial view of Kowloon's uniform apartment blocks, nestled between the trees, gradually began to shallow, until I found myself swallowed up and looking at their dizzying heights from a dual carriageway. I followed my nose to the harbour, weaving through the taxis and pedestrians of the crowded streets, withdrawn, in Kipling's words, 'like a log after a flood'. The city moved fluidly around me, and accepted me into it like wheat into the jaws of a combine harvester. My presence there as a cycle tourist, while incongruous, was easy for this environment, so used to diversification, to accept and digest.

I reflected on how my own ability to accept and welcome alien encounters as they happened had been nurtured by the adventure-cycling experience. I was free and flowing like the city, not just in my ability to ride a bike, pack up a campsite, ascertain a direction or communicate a need, but also in a broader sense, where every problem had a solution, no mountain was too hard to climb and every face was a welcome one. From the situations I had exposed myself to I had gained an array of mental skills and adaptable attitudes that would stay with me for the rest of my days, while the people I had met could be called upon – in my imagination, at least – whenever I needed them. What would a shepherd in rural Turkey say? What

BUDGETING FOR A TOUR

Budgeting will depend on the type, location and duration of the tour you set out on, as well as whether the budget defines the tour, or the tour defines the budget. A week's touring in the Swiss Alps, during which you travel light and depend on your card for food, hotels and everything else will probably be more expensive than living off of noodles and camping for a month in Central Asia. But if you only have a week, don't like camping and really want to go to the Swiss Alps, then the costs will justify themselves. If you have a certain budget and want to get the most out of it, it pays to be open-minded about your destination and frugal with the money you do have. Either way, there are costs that are usually pretty fixed and unavoidable, such as obtaining a bike and the gear you'll need, insurance, visas and flights, as well as the more flexible day-to-day expenses.

There is a school of thought that says you can make do with whatever you have at your disposal, from an old town bike with rusty gears to a musty army sleeping bag with holes in it. While there is a lot of truth in this, if you can afford it, spending a bit of money on a reliable bike, a decent down jacket and comfortable sleeping bag will be worth it. **For shorter tours, you might consider using the services of companies like Pannier.cc, which has a range of cycle-touring gear for hire. For longer tours, you'll need to buy a cycle-touring setup yourself, which can add up. When spending, remind yourself what's important to help you** decide where your money goes: £100 ($133) saved on a new coat could mean funds for an extra week on the road. But £100 spent on a new coat could also let you enjoy your surroundings to the full (or, indeed, keep you alive) – also worth considering, and a reminder that all expenses are contextual. Once you've got your bike and your gear, and with overheads like hotels and transport largely negated, the costs of adventure cycling quickly begin to diminish. The biggest day-to-day expense is food, which will vary greatly between countries. In Europe or the US, the cheapest way of eating is usually to raid the shelves of the local supermarket and cook everything yourself, while in most of Asia and elsewhere, restaurants offer better food, for less money.

Costs from the road:
Hostel in Europe: £16 ($20) a night
Food (pasta, bread, jam, sardines, biscuits, the occasional coffee) in Europe: £4–8 ($5–10) a day
Tea in Turkey: less than 50p (60¢)
Accommodation in Central Asia: £8–12 ($10–15) a night
Accommodation in India: (*dhaba*) £1.50 ($2) a night; (hotel) £11 ($15) a night
Meal in India: 80p–£2.30 ($1–3)
Meal in China: 80p–£3 ($1–4)
Visas: £790 ($1,000)
Flight home: £395 ($500)
Fee to send bike home separately: £160 ($200)

DOCUMENTING CYCLING JOURNEYS

Since the dawn of exploratory adventure, travellers have kept records of their journeys. It is natural to want to document experiences when they are so rich and different, and writing about them or taking photos enables us to gain a new perspective. After you've returned home, such records can also provide a moment of escapism, catapulting you back to the moment in which a photo was taken, or a sentence was scribbled. Here's how to approach it:

Try not to let documenting it overtake the adventure itself, so that you lose perspective on the experience. Live the adventure through your own eyes and ears, not through a lens, microphone or keypad. **DSLR cameras are heavy, expensive and sometimes hideously inconspicuous, so be sure the higher-quality images will be worth it before making space for one.** Smartphones, with their compact size and quick recharge time, as well as their ability to double up as a camera, edit photos, store documents and instantly upload data, cover a lot of bases. Use them to your advantage, but don't rely on them to your disadvantage.

For longer journeys, think about digital storage. Do you need a laptop? Can you get by with just a hard drive and card reader, using a computer when you find one? Think about what you want to create a record of. Is it your trip itself, the place you're travelling through, the people you meet or a combination of the above? **If you plan on keeping a diary, try writing at the start of the day. Come bedtime, your body and brain will be too tired to write anything worthwhile.** You might not always be able to ask if you can take someone's photo, but you can always be respectful. Interacting with a person on some level is not just enjoyable, but will also result in better portraits.

When taking photos of fellow cyclists, expect to do a lot of sprinting up the road to position yourself in advance of photo opportunities. And when taking self-timed photos, expect to do a lot of riding back and forth to set up and collect the camera for every shot. **Be aware of the images you have stored on devices. Officials in certain countries have been known to root through electronics, and the discovery of photos of border fences, government buildings or anything militarial can have serious consequences.**

would the homeless kids in India think? What would be more important to a resident of the Uzbek desert? How would these people feel if they were stood on the shores of Victoria Harbour, looking out across the water to the skyline beyond?

I had arrived. The dark rising shapes and twinkling lights of Hong Kong Island stood across the water, like the very archetype of a modern-day city. The lack of space, the throngs of people, the chaotic traffic, the urgency, materialism, routine, suffocation; hundreds of thousands of bubbles, each with a person inside, streaming across the island of concrete and glass. It was a beautiful thing to look at from the other side of the bay. The skyscrapers, tall and mighty, emanated something of the mountain sublime, while the physical nature of the island seemed symbolic of what it represented: the city – modern life – very much adrift from the experience of adventure that the Eurasian mainland had given me.

Escaping the city by bike can obviously be taken in a very literal sense, as so many of us live in them, and because the disparity in environments between cities and the great outdoors beyond are so great. It is by acknowledging the city's metaphorical island, with its complexities and busyness, as the essence of modern-day life, and the peace of the wild spaces away from that island, that the true benefit of cycle touring is realized. 'In the desert I had found a freedom unattainable in civilization,' wrote Wilfred Thesiger in *Arabian Sands*, 'a life unhampered by possessions, since everything that was not a necessity was an encumbrance.'

When I boarded the ferry to Hong Kong Island, it marked the end of my trip across Eurasia, a year on the road, 26 countries, and roughly 21,000 km (13,050 miles) of Planet Earth. And while the towering buildings of the financial district, uniform residential blocks of the Mid-Levels and illuminated retail banners of Causeway Bay were a very real and breathtaking sight from the ferry deck, they were also a representation of the busy, confused, fast-paced world I was about to re-enter.

Behind I was leaving an existence on the bike that is too often neglected in the city, in modern life. It was an existence in which the primordial needs of food, water and safe shelter were remembered as prerequisites to life, comfort and progress, one that had immersed me completely in the landscapes and people that inhabited them, rather than merely bumbling through them. The definitions of achievement, success and opportunity had been recalibrated. And because of the simplicity of life on a bike, there had been a constant sense of measurable, tangible progress, unadulterated by the complexity and never-ending decision-making of my normal life: one road to follow, without signposts, without junctions, leading onwards to the horizon.

Travelling by bike on an adventure between two points, for no other reason than to travel, with no knowledge of what lies between two points and with no objective other than to find out, is a wonderfully pure and rewarding way of spending some time. It doesn't matter if that time is a day excursion, an overnighter, a week-long tour or a multi-month journey, the fundamental nature of adventure cycling holds true. Its myriad avenues of potential – and one road leading to the horizon – are there to realize now, more than ever.

RIGHT The explosion of life that is Dhaka, Bangladesh. It is also known as the 'rickshaw capital of the world', with its over 400,000 rickshaws.

ON P. 233
A muggy, subtropical evening in Hechi, China.

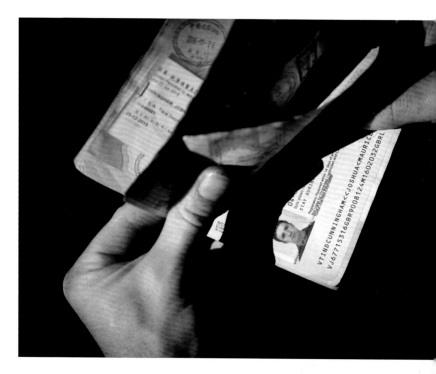

ABOVE On longer bike tours, time in cities is often spent managing passports, visas and the general admin of the road.
RIGHT The comforts, resources and infrastructure of cities make them the ideal places for carrying out bike-maintenance tasks.
LEFT Navigating the chaotic streets of New Delhi.

ABOVE With luggage removed, touring bikes become regular town bikes, and a great way to explore new cities. Outside Hagia Sophia, in Istanbul.

RIGHT My bike receives a thorough inspection from some locals near Dhanbad, India.

OPPOSITE We turn up at a hotel in Baise, China, only to discover it isn't the one we had been told about. Time for a Plan B.

OVERLEAF My Surly 'Cross-Check' at ease in a hostel in Allahabad, India.

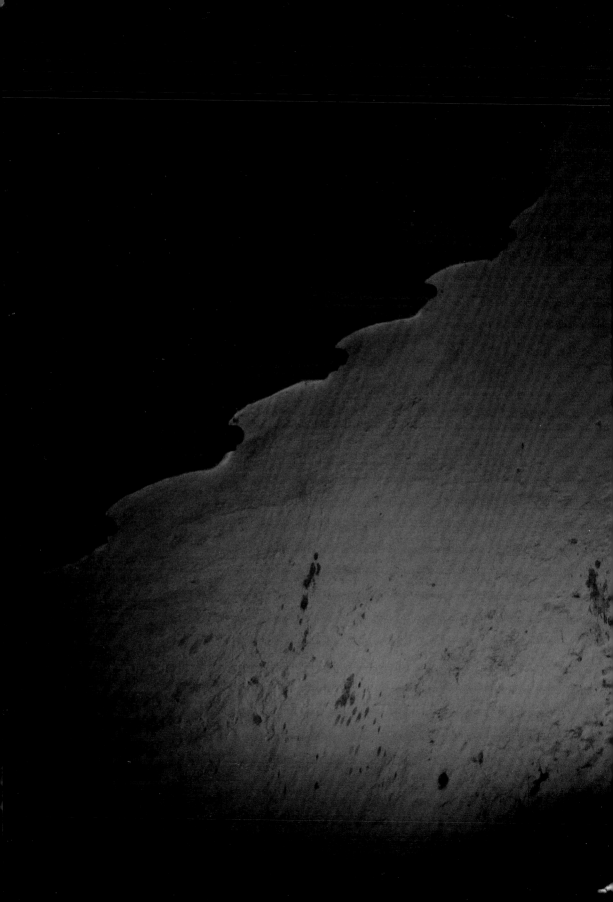

RIGHT Urban areas often require an imaginative approach to wild camping.
BELOW Fellow pedallers, in the form of a gaggle of rickshaw drivers in Bangladesh.
OPPOSITE Jonny negotiating the roads in central Liuzhou, China.
OVERLEAF Searching for a hostel in Guilin, having arrived late in the evening after a long day on the road.

ABOVE Sarajevo provided a haven of warmth and comfort in the middle of a European winter.

RIGHT Pete tends to his bike in Bishkek, Kyrgyzstan, after the mechanical afflictions of the Pamirs.

OPPOSITE Breakfast with Pan, a chance companion of the road for two days in China (above). A cheap, tasty and easy supper at a night market in Phitsanulok, Thailand (below).

OVERLEAF Hitching a ride back towards Bishkek after a challenging few days in the mountains.

ABOVE Threading our way
through traffic on the Grand
Trunk Road in Pakistan.
RIGHT A moment of rest
for both bike and rider in
Khorog, Tajikistan.
OPPOSITE Riding through
a market just after dawn in
Rawalpindi, Pakistan, in search
of a tea stand. A rare moment
of inner-city tranquillity.

ABOVE Ambushed by a paint-wielding crowd at a Holi festival in New Delhi, India.
RIGHT Making conversation with passing traffic in Pakistan.
OPPOSITE Escaping the 40° C (104° F) heat in Gujranwala, Pakistan, with a lunchtime nap at a *dhaba*.
OVERLEAF Where there are people, there's the chance of a treat like these ice lollies, somewhere in China.
ON P. 256 Sleeping in the stairwell of an abandoned petrol station on the outskirts of Lahore, Pakistan.

>

RESOURCES

ONLINE RESOURCES

The number of travelling and adventure cyclists is growing by the day, which means that there are more and more channels through which they can connect. Here are a few to explore:

WARM SHOWERS
warmshowers.org
This network offers one of the biggest communities of touring cyclists. Hosts can be found across Europe and much of the rest of the world, allowing cyclists to pinpoint other users on a map, send messages and ask (politely) for advice on the local area.

COUCHSURFING
couchsurfing.com
Like Warm Showers, anyone can sign up and join a worldwide community of travellers. It's not cycling-exclusive, however, so while there are a lot more people on it, there is also less understanding of cycle tourists' specific needs.

CASA DE CYCLISTAS
cdclatinoamerica.
wordpress.com
Literally 'home of the cyclists', this host and sharing network is similar to Warm Showers, but on a smaller scale, and local only to South America.

CRAZYGUYONABIKE
crazyguyonabike.org
This website is a resource of adventure-cycling legend. Comprising journals, galleries, forums, classifieds and more, all dedicated to cycling journeys worldwide, Crazyguyonabike has long been the go-to place for trip documentation and information-sharing.

INSTAGRAM
instagram.com
A great resource for sparking destination ideas and seeing what the rest of the adventure-cycling community is up to. Some hashtags to get started with:
#worldbybike
#biketouring
#fromwhereiride
#cycletouring
#bikewander
#bikepacking #bikepack
#adventurebybike
#gobybike
#worldontwowheels
#biketrip #bicycletouring
#roadslikethese
#biketravel

FACEBOOK
facebook.com
Facebook is filled with groups, public and private, which are dedicated to cycle-touring. From the all-encompassing 'Bicycle Touring' to the more specific 'Warm Showers Turkey' or 'Silk Road Cycling', it is potentially the greatest resource out there, full of up-to-date advice, information and connectibility with cyclists who are out there doing it, right now.

**THORN TREE
AND TRIPADVISOR**
lonelyplanet.com/
thorntree
tripadvisor.co.uk/
forumhome
Lonely Planet's online forum and Tripadvisor are probably the two biggest communities for travel-related information-sharing. If you're planning on visiting places that don't appear in cycling-specific channels, this is where to find people who have visited them – or at least done some prior research.

CARAVANISTAN
caravanistan.com
If you plan on visiting the Silk Road, this is the place to start. Specializing in the Central Asian '-stan' countries, but also venturing into China, the Caucasus and Turkey, this website has everything you need in one place, from booking tours to information on visas.

**EUROVELO
AND SUSTRANS**
eurovelo.com
sustrans.org.uk
Signposted cycling routes across Europe and around the UK.

FURTHER READING

ADVENTURE CYCLING ASSOCIATION
adventurecycling.org
Founded in 1976, this American organization has a large membership base and offers maps, tours and communication forums.

DANGEROUS ROADS
dangerousroads.org
A website with a comprehensive directory of the world's most spectacular roads. Great for route inspiration.

TRACK MY TOUR
trackmytour.com
Enables users to create a visual story of their travels online, using a map with pin drops and uploaded photos for people to follow.

MAPS.ME
maps.me
Allows users to download chunks of map at a time, making them available offline. Upload KML route files, drop pins, and get directions – and it's free.

BOOKS
T. Allen, *Janapar: Love, on a Bike* (Polegate, East Sussex: Janapar Media, 2013).

N. Crane and R. Crane, *Bicycles up Kilimanjaro*, new ed. (Oxford: Oxford Illustrated Press, 1987).

I. Hibbell, *Into the Remote Places* (London: HarperCollins, 1984).

A. Humphreys, *Moods of Future Joys: Around the World by Bike*, 2nd rev. ed. (Amersham, Buckinghamshire: Eye Books, 2014).

R. Lilwall, *Cycling Home from Siberia* (London: Hodder & Stoughton, 2010).

D. Murphy, *Full Tilt: Ireland to India with a Bicycle* (London: Eland Publishing Ltd, 2010).

N. and H. Pike, *Adventure Cycle-Touring Handbook: Worldwide Cycling Route & Planning Guide*, 2nd ed. (Hindhead, Surrey: Trailblazer Publications, 2010).

H. Stücke, *Home is Elsewhere: Fifty Years Around the World by Bike* (London: Brompton Bicycle Ltd, 2015).

OTHER PUBLICATIONS
Bicycle Traveler magazine
bicycletraveler.
bicyclingaroundtheworld.nl

WEBSITES
adventurecycling.org
bicycletimesmag.com
bicycletouringpro.com
bikepacking.com
bunyanvelo.com
campinmygarden.com
cyclingabout.com
farridemag.com
opencyclemap.org
pannier.cc
ridewithgps.com
tomsbiketrip.com
travellingtwo.com
trustroots.org

FULL KIT LISTS:
BY WEIGHT

LIGHT

Bike
- Multi-tool
- Pump
- Puncture-repair kit
- Tyre levers
- Tyre boots
- Spare inner tubes
- Chain breaker

Camping
- Sleeping bag
- Sleeping-bag liner
- Bivvy bag

Clothing
- Touring SPD shoes
- Socks
- Merino base layer
- Boxer shorts
- Padded cycling shorts
- Waterproof shell jacket
- Down jacket
- Comfy trousers
- Leg/arm warmers
- Buff

Electrical
- Mobile phone
- Plug adaptor
- USB-rechargeable lights
- Bike computer

Miscellaneous
- Head torch
- Basic toiletries
- Basic first-aid kit
- Wallet
- Watch
- Passport and documentation
- Bike helmet

MEDIUM

All of the above, plus the following:

Bike
- Spare chain, brake and gear cables, nuts and bolts, brake pads and spokes
- Quicklink
- 15mm spanner
- Chain lube

Camping
- Foam or inflatable mattress
- Tarp

Cooking
- Stove
- Pot and pan
- Small kitchen knife

Clothing
- Shorts
- T-shirt
- Softshell jacket
- Gilet
- Gloves

Electrical
- Camera
- iPod

Miscellaneous
- Maps
- Torch
- Waterproof bags
- Microfibre towel
- Packable day bag
- Diary and notebook
- Pens and pencils Books

HEAVY

All of the above, plus the following:

Bike
- Lock
- Spare foldable tyre
- Cassette-removal tool
- Spoke key
- Rag
- Bell

Camping
- Tent

Cooking
- Camping cutlery
- Sparking fire stick, waterproof matches, lighter
- Water purifier
- Dromedary bag

Clothing
- Merino long johns
- Waterproof trousers
- Casual trousers
- Cotton shirt
- Fleece
- Flip flops
- Glove liners
- Cycling cap
- Helmet
- Sunglasses

Electrical
- Laptop
- Hard drive
- Speaker
- Solar-power charger

Miscellaneous
- Compass
- Whistle
- Lightweight rope
- Reflective vest
- Arno straps
- Bungee cord
- Zip ties
- Duct tape
- Penknife

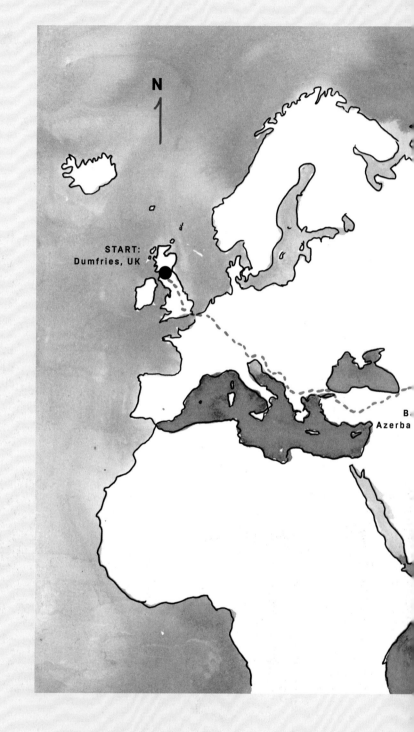

N

START:
Dumfries, UK

B
Azerba

shanbe,
jikistan

New Delhi,
India

Guangzhou,
China

FINISH: Hong Kong

Thank you to all who helped make this journey possible, both at home and on the road.

On the cover: Evening kilometres in the Spiti valley of Himachal Pradesh, northern India.

Escape by Bike: Adventure Cycling, Bikepacking and Touring Off-Road
© 2018 Thames & Hudson Ltd
Text © 2018 Joshua Cunningham
Photographs © 2018 Joshua Cunningham

Illustrations by Chris McNally

Designed by Andrew Diprose

First published in 2018 in the United States of America by
Thames & Hudson Inc., 500 Fifth Avenue, New York, New York 10110

www.thamesandhudsonusa.com

Library of Congress Control Number 2017945429

ISBN 978-0-500-29350-8

Printed and bound in China by C & C Offset Printing Co. Ltd